CONTENTS

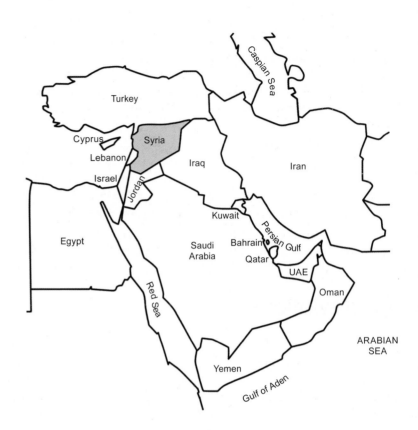

Helion & Company Limited
26 Willow Road, Solihull, West Midlands, B91 1UE, England
Tel. 0121 705 3393
Fax 0121 711 4075

Email: info@helion.co.uk   Website: www.helion.co.uk   Twitter: @helionbooks   Visit our blog http://blog.helion.co.uk/

Published by Helion & Company 2015
Designed and typeset by Kerrin Cocks, SA Publishing Services
Cover designed by Kerrin Cocks, SA Publishing Services
Printed by Henry Ling Ltd, Dorchester, Dorset

Text © Tom Cooper 2015
Monochrome images sourced by the author
Colour profiles © Tom Cooper and Radek Panchartek 2015
Maps drawn by George Anderson © Helion & Company Limited 2015

Cover: Photograph - A loyalist formation of T-62s and T-72s advancing to provide support for Hezbollah units in the Qusayr area in early June 2013. Since this battle, there is less and less of the former Syrian Arab Army (SAA) to be seen on the battlefields of Syria. (via M.P.) Colour profile - A reconstruction of the MiG-23BN (serial number 1679), as seen over Damascus in early 2013, while carrying six FAB-500M-62 general-purpose bombs. Like all locally overhauled MiG-23MFs, Syrian MiG-23BNs are equipped with large boxes containing chaff and flare dispensers, installed on the top of the rear fuselage, on either side of the fin. Inset is the insignia of 'The Works' at Nayrab AB, applied on nearly all aircraft and helicopters that are overhauled there. (Tom Cooper)

ISBN 978-1-910294-10-9

British Library Cataloguing-in-Publication Data.
A catalogue record for this book is available from the British Library.

Acknowledgements

I would like to express my deepest gratitude to a great number of people who have helped me prepare this book, foremost all of my friends in Syria and Iran, no matter where they are right now. They have selflessly – and often at great risk for themselves – shared a wealth of precious results of their own research and helped with establishing contacts to important sources and photographers. Sadly, the ongoing conflict and strict security measures imposed by local governments are imposing serious concerns for security of the persons in question (and that of their families) and not permitting me to mention any names in public.

Additional help was provided by my colleagues Albert Grandolini and Stephane Mantoux from France, and several other researchers from ACIG.info forum, foremost Lukasz Nadolski, who provided very detailed statistics on heavy equipment losses of Syrian government forces since 2011.

My further thanks are going to a number of researchers elsewhere, who kindly helped during some of the research that found its way into this book too, in particular: Martin Smisek in the Czech Republic; Radek Panchartek in Slovakia; Alexandar Hunger in Germany; Group 73 and friends in Egypt; Brigadier-General Ahmad Sadik from Iraq; Dr David Nicolle and Mike Bennet in Great Britain; Tom Long in the USA; Menno van der Wall and Jeroen Nijemeijer from the Netherlands; and Robert Szombati from Hungary. Together with my wife, who is always providing all the support and patience I can ask for, all of them have my special thanks for making this book possible.

Abbreviations

4WD	four-wheel drive
AA	anti-aircraft
AB	air base
AFB	Air Force Base (used for US Air Force bases)
AK	Russian for Automat Kalashnikova; general designation for a class of Soviet or former Eastern Bloc-manufactured class of 7.62mm calibre assault rifles
An	Antonov (the design bureau led by Oleg Antonov)
APC	armoured personnel carrier
ATGM	anti-tank guided missile
Brig Gen	brigadier-general
Capt	captain
CO	commanding officer
Col	colonel
ELINT	electronic intelligence
Gen	general
HQ	headquarters
IAP	international airport
IFV	infantry fighting vehicle
Il	Ilyushin (the design bureau led by Sergey Vladimirovich Ilyushin, also known as OKB-39)
IR	infra-red, electromagnetic radiation longer than deepest red light sensed as heat
IRI	Islamic Republic of Iran
IRGC	Islamic Revolutionary Guards Corps
KIA	killed in action
Km	kilometre
LAAF	Libyan Arab Air Force
Lt	lieutenant
Lt Col	lieutenant colonel
1st Lt	first lieutenant
2nd Lt	second lieutenant
Maj	major
Maj Gen	major general
MANPADS	man-portable air defence system(s) – light surface-to-air missile system that can be carried and deployed in combat by a single soldier
MBT	main battle tank
Mi	Mil (Soviet/Russian helicopter designer and manufacturer)
MiG	Mikoyan i Gurevich (the design bureau led by Artyom Ivanovich Mikoyan and Mikhail I osifovich Gurevich, also known as OKB-155 or MMZ' 'Zenit')
NCO	non-commissioned officer
PoW	prisoner of war
RPG	rocket-propelled grenade
SAM	surface-to-air missile
SIGINT	signals intelligence
Su	Sukhoi (the design bureau led by Pavel Ossipowich Sukhoi, also known as OKB-51)
SyAA	Syrian Arab Army
SyAAF	Syrian Arab Air Forces
Technical	improvised fighting vehicle (typically an open-backed civilian 4WD modified to a gun truck)
USSR	Union of Soviet Socialist Republics (or Soviet Union)

1
BACKGROUND

I have travelled extensively around Syria and have maintained relations with many Syrians since my youth. Of those not killed in the meantime, some have been imprisoned since the mid-2000s; others, meanwhile, joined the insurgency, and a few are fighting on the government's side. Due to my research about various air forces in the Middle East over the last decades, I came into the unusual position of being in contact with a significant number of people from countries and military services that became involved in the Syrian Civil War. Even so, it is hard to convey the impact of what was originally known as the 'Syrian Uprising' and meanwhile evolved into a full-blown Syrian Civil War.

Erupting as a conventional popular uprising against an oppressive government, this conflict is much more than what is often seen as a clash between a 'despotic but laicist government and Islamic extremism'. In fact, this war is gradually developing into a major clash waged by a dictatorship of the Syrian Alawite minority – strongly supported by the government of the Islamic Republic of Iran (IRI) and a variety of its proxies, including the Hezbollah (also 'Hizbullah' or 'Hizballah'; a Shi'a political party and militant group from Lebanon) and Russia, on one side – against a conglomerate of native insurgent groups supported by a host of foreign powers (primarily Arab countries of the Persian Gulf), on the other. Although already destroying large parts of major Syrian cities, dozens of towns and hundreds of villages; although bitterly dividing not only the Syrian population but much of the Middle East and beyond; and although sending millions of people into ruinous exile while bringing some of the worst images in recent history to the surface, this merciless, savage and ugly conflict is still going on.

Exact cost in lives remains unknown. At the time this report is written, various non-government-organisations (NGOs) are estimating the number of deaths caused by illness and malnutrition at around 200,000, while another 140,000 could have been killed in fighting. Less than half of the confirmed deaths may have been combatants from both sides: civilians are suffering so much that nearly 8 million Syrians have become displaced, of which about 2 million fled to neighbouring countries. At least as tragic are estimates for the number of people missing or assumed as detained – primarily by the government – variously reported at between 60,000 and 130,000. Beyond these tragic figures, it is impossible to reasonably assess the economic and material damage for the country, except to conclude that Syria is ruined and unlikely to recover as a sovereign and functioning country for decades to come.

Although often languishing on the brink of reporting by mass media, the Syrian Civil War is one of the most publicised conflicts in the history of humankind. Due to the widespread availability of the internet and social media, observers are in a position to follow the events almost as if peeking over the shoulder of many of the involved combatants. However, it is also one of the most politicised conflicts ever, and a war characterised by an unprecedented spread of misinformation and propaganda.

The following account is an attempt to dissect military-related developments and combat operations in Syria in the period between

The entrance to the ruins of Ugarit, a Neolithic town that maintained trade connections to Cyprus, Egypt and the valleys of the Euphrates and Tigris rivers. (Photo by Tom Cooper)

The Great Colonnade in the ruins of Apamea, once a prosperous Roman town in the Orontes River Valley, about 55km north-west of Hama. (Photo by Tom Cooper)

The Roman amphitheatre in Bosra (also known as Busra ash-Sham), a UNESCO World Heritage Site. (Photo by Tom Cooper)

early 2011 and late 2013 from 'ambient sounds', and to record and summarise what became known about the war itself. Although some descriptions of geo-political circumstances are provided, these are kept to an absolute minimum and are primarily used to explain the backgrounds to certain developments. Furthermore, I have purposefully avoided discussing possible Western military interventions and involvement, and entering in-depth discussions about deployment of chemical weapons by forces loyal to the Syrian government. While the former never happened during the period covered by this book, the deployment of chemical weapons remains mired in much controversy and was primarily aiming to hit civilians in insurgent-held areas, in turn having next to no effects upon developments on the battlefield.

That said, I would like to stress that my reporting about this conflict is not only certain to contain mistakes, which are all mine, but is also biased. I find there is no doubt about causes for this war; no doubt about who turned it into an inter-ethnic and inter-religious strife; and even less doubt about who is prolonging the bloodshed and agony and turning large parts of beautiful Syria into a wasteland through internationalising this conflict.

SYRIA THROUGH THE CENTURIES

Positioned in the centre of the Fertile Crescent and the Middle East, on the vital crossroads between Africa, Asia and Europe, the area nowadays within Syria's borders experienced some of the earliest human inhabitation and the emergence of several of the earliest civilisations. The oldest remains found in Syria date from the Palaeolithic era, approximately 800,000 BC. Remains of Neanderthals who lived there in the Middle Palaeolithic era (circa 200,000 to 40,000 years ago) were found, as were the ruins of numerous early cities from the late Neolithic era and Bronze Age. There is an ongoing debate over whether the Phoenician or Ugaritic alphabet – the latter named after the ancient port city of Ugarit, 11 kilometres north of the modern port city of Lattakia – was the first ever, while Damascus, the capital of Syria, is one of the oldest sites of permanent human inhabitation. Ugarit was part of an empire that may have stretched from Anatolia in modern-day Turkey, east to Mesopotamia and south to the Red Sea, around 3,000 BC, and that traded with the Mesopotamian states of Sumer Akkad and Assyria, and with Egypt. Subsequently, various parts of this area were successively occupied by Sumerians,

Egyptians, Hittites, Assyrians and Babylonians, Canaanites and Phoenicians, Arameans and Amorites, the Neo-Assyrian Empire and then by Persians in 539 BC. Alexander the Great ended the Persian dominance in 333–332 BC and subsequently the area was incorporated into the Seleucid Empire, the capital of which was Antioch, nowadays inside Turkey. The Roman general Pompey the Great captured Antioch in 64 BC, turning Syria into a Roman Province. During the time of the Roman Empire, Antioch became a major centre of trade and industry, and the third biggest city, after Rome and Alexandria – despite a brief contest with the powerful indigenous Aramean state, centred around Palmyra, in the 2nd and 3rd Centuries AD.

The area became part of the East Roman, or Byzantine, Empire in AD 395, but was conquered by the Muslim Arabs of the Rashidun Army – led by Khalid Ibn al-Wallid – between AD 634 and 640, to become a part of the Islamic Empire. The Umayyad dynasty – which expanded this empire from Spain to India – placed its capital in Damascus, and Syria prospered immensely. Christians, mostly ethnic Arameans, present in the area already since Paul the Apostle was converted on the road to Damascus, were completely equal to Moslems and held important governmental posts. Indeed, Greek and Aramaic languages remained dominant even after Umayyads made Arabic the official language. The Caliphate collapsed over dynastic struggles and religious disputes in the mid-8th Century, and the Abbasid dynasty then moved the capital of the empire to Baghdad. The Byzantines returned to recapture most of the area in the 10th Century, but Syria then experienced a period of great turmoil, becoming a battleground between the Byzantine Empire, the Damascus-based Fatimid dynasty, the Buyids of Baghdad, Seljuk Turks and Crusaders, who arrived in the late 11th Century and committed countless atrocities against the local population before establishing several of their own states. Few Crusader states survived the conquests by Saladin (Salah ad-Din), the founder of the Ayyubid dynasty of Egypt, until in 1260 the Mongols briefly swept through Syria. The withdrawal of the Mongols was followed by an invasion by the Mamluks of Egypt. Mamluk Sultan Baibars destroyed the last of the Crusader footholds and made Damascus a provincial capital, but this period of reconstruction experienced a tragic end during the invasion of the Tamerlanes, led by Timur Lenk, in 1400, which massacred much of the population and deported most of the survivors to

An overview of the ruins in Palmyra, once a powerful Arabic city in central Syria, near modern-day Tadmor. (Photo by Tom Cooper)

One of 17 *norias*, ancient water wheels used for irrigation purposes in the Hama area since Roman times. (Photo by Fabian Hinz)

The Crusades have left a lasting trace on the landscape of Syria. Fortresses like the famous Krak de Chevaliers (formerly the Crac de l'Ospital), one of the most important preserved medieval castles in the world, were constructed on the hilltops of the anti-Lebanon mountain chain along the current border with Lebanon every 20–40 kilometres. (Photo by Tom Cooper)

The statue of Saladin, (Kurdish) Ayyubid Sultan, at the western entrance to the Citadel of Damascus. (Photo by Fabian Hinz)

Samarkand. By 1516, when Syria was conquered by the Ottoman Empire, the area had also lost its importance due to the discovery of a sea route from Europe to the Fast East, and for a while degenerated to a transit point on the route to Mecca.

Under Ottoman administration, Syria was reorganised into one large province – or eyelet – consisting of several districts (sanjaks) in which each religious minority had its own religious head and was administered by its own laws and certain civil functions. A peaceful coexistence among the meanwhile very different sections of local society was fostered over the following 400 years, and Eyelet Syria – which included modern-day Syria, Lebanon, Israel/Palestine, Jordan and sizeable parts of Iraq and Turkey – experienced significant economic growth towards the end of the 19th Century.

THE KINGDOM OF SYRIA AND FRENCH OCCUPATION

Much of what is going on in Syria today was pre-determined by the turbulent history of the Middle East since the late 19th Century. A series of local uprisings against Ottoman rule resulted in the development of a sense of loyalty to Arabic history within intellectual circles of modern-day Syria and Lebanon of that time. A number of emerging Arab nationalist organisations of different political- and religious-orientation surfaced that became influential because of their demands for social and political reforms, independence from the Ottoman Empire and unity for all Arab territories. Although some of the leading figures from these organisations, as well as traditional leaders from other parts of the Arab world, eventually gained some influence in Istanbul, dissent continued to grow. During the First World War, Arabs established ties to the British, who made promises of independence in return for an Arab uprising against the Ottomans. Correspondingly, Faisal Ibn Hussein, son of Sharif Hussein Ibn Ali of Mecca, then the ruler of Hejaz (nowadays Western Province of Saudi Arabia), launched the Arab Revolt, in 1916, better known to Westerners for the involvement of British Army officer Thomas E Lawrence (Lawrence of Arabia). After a two-year campaign, Faisal's insurgent forces followed the Egyptian Expeditionary Forces (primarily consisting of units from various parts of the British Commonwealth), led by General Edmund Allenby, into Damascus in late September 1918.

However, at the same time that the government in London was making promises to Sharif Hussein, it reached separate agreements with the French – including the Sykes-Picot Agreement – aiming to distribute the Ottoman Empire between them. Therefore, while the Arabs subsequently declared an independent Kingdom of Syria 'in its natural boundaries' – from the Taurus mountains in Turkey to the Sinai desert in Egypt, and including large parts of modern-day northern Iraq, most of modern-day Jordan and even some of modern-day Saudi Arabia – the French found this development completely unacceptable. Ignoring the findings of the US-sponsored King-Crane Commission (set up to determine the wishes of local inhabitants in 1919), and the official declaration of the Kingdom of Syria as the first modern and sovereign Arab state, on 8 March 1920, the French landed troops in Lebanese ports and imposed an ultimatum upon Faisal – to fight or capitulate. While Faisal surrendered, his Minister of Defence, Yusuf al-Azma, led a small Army to confront the invasion, but was easily defeated at the Battle of Maysalun in July 1920. Following the siege and capture of Damascus, Paris imposed the French Mandate for Syria and the Lebanon, on 24 July.[1] During the San Remo Conference later that year, Syria was officially distributed to be a part of a French mandate, including modern-day Syria and Lebanon, with Palestine, Transjordan and Iraq under British control.

Ever since, the short-lived Kingdom of Syria – often belittled and disparaged as 'Dreams of Greater Syria' by Israel and the West – has been a subject of great inspiration to many Arabs, foremost as a story of them breaking out from colonial rule only to be betrayed and castigated by Western powers, and then the Jews. Unsurprisingly, considering this and the harsh French rule, it took only a few years before Arabs under the Druze leader Sultan Pasha al-Atrash launched the Great Syrian Revolt in 1925. Early on, al-Atrash's forces – that included insurgents from many different ethnic and religious groups – won several battles. The French reacted by deploying large contingents of colonial troops

One of the few Renault R-35 light tanks left behind by the French, and pressed into service with the nascent Syrian Arab Army (SAA) during the war in Palestine in 1948, as seen in the former Military Museum of Damascus (closed in 2010). (Photo by Tom Cooper)

This Dodge Tanakeh was taken from former Free-French forces and pressed into service with the SyAA in the late 1940s. (Photo by Tom Cooper)

to regain the main cities, and defeating the Arabs in the battles of Msfirah and as-Suwayda, but the revolt was crushed only after a massive bombardment of Damascus, in 1927, in which up to 40,000 Syrians were massacred. Al-Atrash was forced to escape into exile in Jordan. Sentenced to death *in absentia*, he was pardoned and returned to Syria in 1937, and remained involved in politics into the early 1950s, becoming one of the most popular and prominent figures in Syrian history, next to Baibars, and certainly before Saladin.

Political unrest against French rule continued into the 1930s, fostering the ascent of nationalist movements fuelled not only by demands for independence, but also the increasing Jewish immigration to Palestine under the British Mandate. Eventually, Paris was forced to offer independence to Syria, in 1934, but the corresponding treaty was heavily prejudiced in French favour and fiercely opposed by nationalists led by Hashim al-Atassi (former Prime Minister of Faisal's government). Atassi completely renegotiated this agreement and two years later received a tumultuous welcome on his return to Damascus, but popular elation over his success was short-lived: the lingering imperialist inclinations of the French government resulted in Paris reconsidering its promises and never ratifying the new agreement. On the contrary, the British and Zionists added plenty of salt to Syrian wounds by provoking the Arab revolt in Palestine, while the French put the dot on the comma when practically ceding the province of Alexandretta to Turkey, in 1938–1939, and through starting to set up an independent Lebanon. This reignited unrest and mass protesting continued into 1941, when Syria was occupied by the British, followed by Free French forces, in reaction to Nazi encouragement of Arabs (as a counter to British hegemony) and Vichy French authorities granting permission for German aircraft and supplies to transit Syria on the way to Iraq.

Confronted with a Jewish insurgency that made the Mandate increasingly unpopular at home, the British government subsequently attempted a re-establishment of 'Greater Syria' (including Palestine). Despite severe pressure upon General Charles de Gaulle's administration from 1944 onwards, such efforts were prevented by a series of developments that included the Lebanese declaration of independence in 1943 and secret French co-operation with militant Zionist organisations. Even then, it took another French military intervention – including another heavy bombardment of Damascus and countless civilian deaths – and immense international pressure to force Paris to finally release Syria into independence, and withdraw its remaining troops, on 17 April 1946, which was subsequently declared the Independence Day of the Arab Republic of Syria.

INDEPENDENT SYRIA

Despite resulting in a short period of rapid economic development, independence brought no respite to the nascent Syria. It not only proved extremely difficult to govern because of its complex demography, but went through a number of traumatic experiences early on. Syrians never managed to re-establish a union with Lebanon, negotiations for a union with Transjordan failed and soon after they lost the last semblance of control over Palestine. Meanwhile, the civil war between Arabs and Jews in that territory culminated in an outright campaign of ethnic cleansing of the former, in late 1947 and early 1948, and the declaration of an independent Israel, in May 1948, which in turn provoked an invasion by several nations of the Arab League, including Syria. Following nearly a year of bitter fighting, the Arabs were pushed out and forced to accept a UN-negotiated ceasefire, which left Israel in control of nearly all of Palestine bar the Gaza Strip and West Bank. Understood in Syria as a defeat caused by incompetent government officials that resulted in a massive economic loss for the country, that defeat prompted a coup d'état against the democratic rule, in March 1949, followed by two further coups by the end of that year. The military returned the power to civilians following a series of additional coups and a popular uprising, in 1954, but this pattern was to be repeated so often that, by 1958, the country was ruled by no less than 20 different governments and had four separate constitutions.

This latent political instability and the appeal of the leadership of President Gamal Abdel Nasser of Egypt in the wake of the Suez War of 1956 eventually resulted in popular support for a union with Egypt. Therefore, on 1 February 1958, Syria's President Shukri al-Kuwatli and Nasser announced the merger of the two countries, creating the United Arab Republic (UAR). Nasser's

Flags of various branches of the Syrian military: in the centre is the original SyAAF flag (with roundel, in use from 1948 until 1958) and to its right is the current SyAAF flag. (Photo by Tom Cooper)

The ruins of Qunaitra, formerly the capital of the Golan province, captured by Israel in the June 1967 Arab-Israeli War and deliberately and systematically demolished during the Israeli withdrawal in June 1974. (Photo by Tom Cooper)

rule soon turned into a great disappointment for Syrians: while expected to be fair and to share power, and despite countless warnings from his aides, the Egyptian president ordered the disbandment of all political parties, positioned Egyptians in nearly all of the major positions in politics and the military, introduced an Egyptian-style land reform and removed most of Syria's industry and military to Egypt. Unsurprisingly, such decisions and massive mismanagement of the local economy created much resentment and an anti-Egyptian military coup ended the union in 1961. On their own devices, successive Syrian governments attempted rapprochement with the West between 1961 and 1963 and the country experienced a brief period of economic growth before another series of coups resulted in the establishment of the Ba'ath Party's rule in 1964 and friendly relations with the Soviet Union. Political unrest continued, nevertheless, due to continuous power struggles within the Ba'ath Party and the increasingly powerful groups within the minority Alawite sect, further exacerbated by defeat during the June 1967 war with Israel, when Syria lost the prosperous Golan Heights (pronounced Jawlan in Syria).

THE RISE OF ALAWITES

Alawites are a group frequently – yet erroneously – categorised as a 'Shi'a sect'. They had diverged from the mainstream Twelver of the Imami branch of Shi'a Islam in the 9th Century, but nowadays the only link between them and Shi'a Islam stems from their reverence for the Prophet Muhammad's cousin and son-in-law, Ali. Indeed, modern-day Alawites have many things in common with Christians and are as often shunned by the Sunnis and Shi'a alike. Because of their 'heresy' and rejection of Sharia Law, celebration of many Christian holidays and revering of Christian saints, the sect remained impoverished over the centuries and became secretive. Furthermore, considering their history as a fractious bunch divided among rival tribes, many Alawites began embracing the Shi'a concept of taqqiya (concealing or assimilating one's faith to avoid prosecution) while dealing with Sunnis.

The rise of Alawites in Syria began during the French rule of the 1920s, when they were – together with other minorities – legitimised and supported by Mandate authorities as a counterweight to the Sunnis. They not only enjoyed subsidies,

legal rights and lower taxes than their Sunni counterparts, but were recruited into the military (the Troupes Speciale du Levant), police and intelligence services in an attempt to suppress Sunni challenges to French rule and create a quasi-state within the Mandate.

The Sunnis and even Christians quickly reasserted their political power and sidelined Alawites from civilian authorities in the 1950s, but – while occupying the top posts in the armed forces – they overlooked the heavy presence of Alawites in the lower ranks.[2] The seed was thus planted not only for an Alawite-led military, but also for the rise of the Ba'ath party (rapidly filled with Alawites), which campaigned for secularism, socialism, Arab nationalism and Alawite migration into the cities. Following the coup of 1963, Ba'athist President Amin al-Hafiz discharged many ranking Sunni officers, providing openings for hundreds of Alawites to top-tier military positions. At the same time, heavy recruitment among Alawi communities further exacerbated the earlier trend, with some units becoming overwhelmingly staffed by this sect. Before long, the Alawites began laying their claim to the Syrian state and Alawite Major General Salah Jadid imposed himself as the de-facto Syrian strongman, instead of the President of the Republic, actually a ceremonial figurehead, Dr Nureddin al-Atassi.

Together with the militant Leninist Jadid, it was another top Alawite officer – the then Minister of Defence and Commander of the Syrian Arab Air Force (SyAAF), Major General Hafez al-Assad – who was blamed for the defeat during the June 1967 Arab-Israeli War. Narrowly surviving the crisis, Assad began consolidating his position in the military establishment and to differ with Jadid because of the latter's radical policies. Following a period of power struggle, Assad's moment came after the failed Syrian military intervention in the Jordanian Civil War of September 1970. Although subsequently stripped of his government post, he deployed the military in a bloodless coup that resulted in the arrest of leading members of the detested Jadid's administration and all of Assad's internal enemies. On 16 November 1970, Hafez al-Assad declared himself as prime minister. After firmly establishing himself in power, three years later he institutionalised his position through declaring himself the President of the Arab Republic of Syria.

POPULATION AND GEOGRAPHY

The country that came under Assad's rule is usually considered as populated by 'Arabs'. Actually, its population – nowadays estimated at between 22.5 and 23.5 million – consists of a blend of people of very diverse ethnic and religious backgrounds. The volatility that generally accompanies sectarianism resulted in the government deliberately avoiding conducting censuses on the religious demographic, making it difficult to determine the exact composition of religious majorities and minorities, which is why only rough estimates about this issue are available. Most of these assess the Syrian population as 70-75 percent Sunni Muslim (including Arabs and Kurds), up to 15 percent other Muslims (including Alawites, Ismailis, Shi'a and Druze) and about 10 percent Christian (Orthodox and Maronite), while other minorities include a few Jewish communities that were still present in Aleppo and Damascus in 2010. Sunni Arabs make up roughly 60 percent of the population, together with Sunni Kurds (approximately nine percent) and Sunni Turkomen (three percent), and there are significant minorities of (Christian) Syriac-Armaic people and Assyrians (up to about 2.5 million), Armenians (approximately 100,000), Indo-European Christians, Circassians, Yazidis, Greeks, Mandeans, Jews and others. Furthermore, about 400,000 Palestinian Arab refugees (many of them Christians) and at least 1.3 million (some of the Syrian estimates went as high as three million during the mid-2000s) Iraqi refugees used to live in Syria as of early 2011, although many of them are understood to have left the country since. The official language is Arabic, of which several dialects are spoken in everyday life, but many other languages are spoken among the minorities, and most educated Syrians speak English, French and German, while Russian is spoken by most military officers.

The Syrian population is usually assessed as quite young, with more than 90 percent being younger than 60. The local culture is traditionalist, generally placing greatest importance upon family, education, religion, self-discipline, respect and welcoming of guests. Except for many Arabs considering Syria as the cradle of their civilisation, Damascus is traditionally one of the most important Arab cultural centres, especially in the field of classic Arab music, while Aleppo is renowned for Andalous sung poetry. In recent years, Syrian soap operas were quite successful throughout the eastern Arab world.

Syria's geography and climate are as diverse as its population. Although large swathes of the country – especially the area between Homs, ar-Raqqah, Dayr az-Zawr and the border to Iraq – are sparsely populated, only about 55 percent of the total population is living in urban centres. Aleppo is the biggest city, usually assessed as having a population of between 2 and 3 million; Damascus is populated by at least 1.7 million, possibly up to 6 million including suburbs and the surrounding Rif Dimashq Province; Homs used to have a population of about 1.3 million, and Hama about 850,000. Sadly, much of this has changed since the start of the war.

The geography consists of the narrow, densely populated, humid and fertile coastal plain stretching from the Turkish border to Lebanon. Rain in this area is fairly abundant, mostly falling between November and May. Towards the east, the coastal plain climbs into the Jabal an-Nusayriyah, a mountain range with an average elevation of around 1,200 metres extending parallel to

Illustrating the diverse landscape of Syria, this is a view from the Anti-Lebanon Mountains towards the east, showing 'Syria's granary', the Orontes River Valley north of Hama. The snow caps in these mountains melt away only in April and May. (Photo by Tom Cooper)

the coastal plain. At the southern end of the Jabal an-Nusayriyah is the Homs Gap, a favourite trade and invasion route from the coast to the country's interior, but also a densely populated area with intensive agriculture, that often receives rain-bearing clouds from the Mediterranean. East of the mountain range is the Orontes River Valley, a fertile and intensively cultivated area. Further south, the Anti-Lebanon Mountains rise to peaks of over 2,700 metres along the border with Lebanon, that have little rainfall and merge with the desert. At the south-west end of this mountain chain is Mount Jabal ash-Sheikh (Mount Hermon), on the southern slopes of which are the green and water-rich Golan Heights, since June 1967 Arab-Israeli War occupied by Israel, and since 1981 annexed by it in an act that was never accepted by Syria, nor recognised by the international community.

At the joint of the Anti-Lebanon Mountains and the central plateau lies Damascus, a former oasis overlooked by Mount Kasyun. Although lying in the semi-arid climatic zone of the steppe, it is verdant and cultivable because of irrigation from the Barada River (primarily by aqueducts built during Roman times). East of the Golan Heights and south of Damascus is the Hawran Plateau, characterised by volcanic cones that intersperse the otherwise open, rolling terrain, and further south-east is the high volcanic region of the Jabal ad-Druze (now renamed the Jabal al-Arab). However, most of the country consists of the eastern plateau, a region of hard-packed dirt surface intersected by a low chain of mountains that extend north-eastwards to the Euphrates. South of the mountains is the barren gravel desert region known as Hamad, while north of it is the Homs Desert. North-eastern Syria is characterised by its dependence on the Euphrates River (which provides more than 80 percent of water resources for the entire country), the banks of which are densely populated and intensively cultivated.

A COUP-PROOF GOVERNMENT

Hafez al-Assad ruled such a complex country through extremely careful integration of the Alawites into the military and security apparatus, and integration of the military into the government. He vastly expanded internal security services and established a powerful network of informants all through Syrian society, eventually

A view of north-western Damascus, with Mount Qasioun in the background. Largely constructed since independence, this part of the Syrian capital is the power base of the Assad government. Beyond Qasioun, on the left side of this photo, is a complex of bases housing the Republican Guards Division, stretching for nearly 20 kilometres. (Photo by Tom Cooper)

creating several para-military organisations, the primary purpose of which was securing his rule – such as the Defence Companies (Saraya ad-Difa, SAD), commanded by Hafez's brother Rifa'at al-Assad. In the process of this reform, and although a staunch anti-communist, Assad signed a friendship treaty with Moscow and granted a limited influx of Soviet instructors in exchange for vast quantities of modern arms. His war for liberation of the Golan Heights, launched in October 1973 in co-operation with Egypt, was not successful, but during subsequent ceasefire negotiations he did manage to force the Israelis to make limited concessions. They withdrew from a narrow strip on the eastern side of the Golan Heights and ceded it to Syria, albeit not before completely demolishing the former administrational, commercial and tourism centre of the area, the town of Quneitra.

Although Hafez al-Assad's dogged secularism won the backing of religious minorities, the combination of accusations over the Ba'ath Party's betrayal in the June 1967 war, lack of success during the October 1973 war and Assad's removal of a clause from the Syrian constitution – according to which the president had to be a Moslem – put him at odds with Syrian Sunnis. Some of these were organised into the Syrian Moslem Brotherhood (MB) – which in Syria had existed since the late 1930s and used to represent an influential political party in the 1950s – the military wing of which decided to launch an insurgency in the late 1970s, amid many quarrels with the rest of this organisation and other Sunni movements. Sponsored by the government of Jordan (possibly also that of Saudi Arabia), the uprising reached its peak with an attack on the Aleppo Artillery School, on 16 June 1979, in which 83 cadets were killed. Subsequently, daily terrorist attacks gradually spread around the country. Not all of these were undertaken by the Brotherhood: the resistance did gain some popular support and spread well beyond areas usually associated with that organisation. Indeed, the Islamic Revolution in Iran motivated a wave of mass protests and strikes that spread through Syria in 1980, some of which degenerated into fire fights with security forces.

With all of the security apparatus and most of the military dominated by Alawites, Assad's government found it unproblematic to react with brutal suppression. In February 1980, Assad ordered the 3rd Armoured Division and the SADs into Aleppo. Mechanised units sealed off entire districts, and then commandos launched house-by-house raids, rounding up hundreds of suspects. Similar practices were applied in Hama and Dera'a a few weeks later, causing the death of hundreds of those in oppositional – whether Moslem Brothers or not – and thousands arrested. The MB attempted to assassinate al-Assad on 26 June 1980, but failed and the Syrian president ordered the summary execution of around 1,000 Moslem Brothers held in the notorious prison in Palmyra/Tadmor.[3]

Theoretically, the insurgency was thus crushed: but in practice, the brutal reaction of security services prompted much of the Brotherhood into further radicalisation – which in turn facilitated its downfall, because extremist Islamism does not traditionally find much sympathy from the Syrian public. After small-scale attacks against government and military objects in Damascus and elsewhere did not bring the desired effects, on 2 February 1982 the MB launched a major insurrection in Hama. While successful in bringing the city under their control and murdering a number of leading Alawites, they did not gain widespread support. The government thus found it easy to put down the revolt. Surrounded by elements of the 47th Armoured and 21st Mechanised Brigades of the 3rd Division (under the command of Hafez al-Assad's cousin, Major General Shafiq Fayyad), and Rifa'at's SADs, the city was subjected to intensive artillery shelling. After days of massive barrages, commandos and mechanised infantry, supported by tanks, moved in, razing entire districts and slaughtering around 20,000 civilians. By the end of this 'battle', about a third of the historic inner city of Hama had been reduced to rubble. Most of the victims of the assault were buried in mass graves, upon which apartment buildings, public parks and various government facilities were constructed. Although the 3rd A Dremained to garrison the city for a whole year, with a literal 'tank in almost every street', for all practical purposes the Hama massacre ended with a clear-cut defeat of the Brotherhood and the end of the concept of armed insurgency against the Assad regime. While a few surviving Brothers fled abroad, after such a negative experience it took nearly two generations for an entirely new, secular and non-violent opposition to come into being inside Syria.

CROWN-PRINCE'S SPRING

Following years of his reign characterised by the support of several militant Palestinian organisations, close co-operation with the Islamic Republic of Iran and the Hezbollah in Lebanon, and opposition to pro-Western Arab countries, Hafez al-Assad died on 10 June 2000. Because his oldest son Bassel – the 'crown-prince' originally prepared to succeed him on the throne – was killed in a car crash in 1994, Hafez was succeeded by his second son, Bashar Hafez al-Assad. The process of succession posed a significant threat not only for the al-Assad clan, but also the unity of Alawites and the entire government. Unsurprisingly, Hafez al-Assad had already ordered his Army Chief of Staff, Lieutenant General Hikhmat Shihabi, to purge the military and security apparatus of all officers of suspect loyalty in 1998. From what little is known about subsequent developments, it is usually said that only the loyalty of their key Sunni supporters – foremost being the clan of the Sunni Minister of Defence, Mustafa Tlass, supported by

In line with maintenance of the personal cult about Hafez al-Assad, this memorial was erected at the eastern entrance of Quneitra, as a reminder of the Israeli withdrawal in June 1974. Similar memorials and sculptures of al-Assad have been erected in hundreds of other sites around the country. (Photo by Tom Cooper)

A typical poster of Bashar al-Assad, presenting him as a tough military leader – as often seen all over Syria in the 2000s. (Photo by Tom Cooper)

The Al-Assad family, with Hafez al-Assad and his wife Anisa in the foreground, Maher al-Assad (one of the commanders of the Republican Guards Division) standing first from the left, Bashar, Bassel, Majid and Bushra.

Saudis – assured the military's support for the new president.

Educated in the West, Bashar was seen by many as a potential reformer of the police state he inherited from his father. At least initially, he did try different strategies, including releasing political prisoners, closing a few prisons and encouraging something like an 'intellectual debate'. However, this 'Damascus Spring', as it was called, proved short-lived and by 2001 a new wave of repression put the lid on all resentment. Syria remained largely isolated on the international scene. Nevertheless, Bashar did reach reasonable levels of popularity within wide circles of the Syrian public, partly because of repeated increases in pay for public employees and his populist speeches. Furthermore, Syria experienced a gradual economic improvement during the early 2000s, primarily thanks to profits from oil exports and partially because of Saudi investment in local infrastructure. What is less well-known is that many of these Syrian oil exports were actually exports of oil smuggled in from Iraq, which found itself under a set of stringent embargoes during the 1990s. Latecomers into this business (behind Turkey and Iran), the Syrian government began earning nice profits from re-selling Iraqi oil, especially once

Bashar al-Assad wearing the uniform of a 3-star General (the top military rank, not assigned to any other commissioned military officers). (SANA)

the old pipeline connecting Kirkuk with Tartus (constructed by the British in the 1930s) was re-opened. Under pressure to sell in order to earn income required to maintain itself in power, the government of President Saddam Hussein of Iraq was exporting its oil to Syria at discount prices. Damascus sold part of it on the domestic market while exporting the majority at the usual prices. Nobody knows exactly how much Iraqi oil was smuggled via Syria in those years, but some estimates went as high as US$3 billion annually. Syria is not as oil-rich as it neighbours and – buried deep underground – the local oil is expensive to exploit. The smuggling of Iraqi oil had positive effects upon the development of a local petrochemical industry: with the help of income obtained in this fashion, the business of exploiting local oilfields became profitable enough to bridge the gap until the time that oil prices increased enough to make exploitation of Syrian oilfields profitable.

Coupled with limited economic liberalisation, the introduction of private banking, encouragement of foreign private investment and negotiations for a free trade association with the European Union (EU), oil exports resulted in a dampening of demographic pressure. However, many of the positive effects of this development were neutralised by an influx of millions of Iraqi refugees, drought and the Southern Lebanon War of 2006. Ultimately, because of widespread corruption and nepotism, and a continuous brutal repression of any kind of dissent, Syria was in no better position in 2010 than 10 years before.

2
GOVERNMENT FORCES

The armed forces of the Arab Republic of Syria as they existed in 2011 were a result of past confrontations with Israel and an emphasis on maintaining internal security: there was a massive conventional military, including an Army, air force, navy and air defence force. What is less well-known is the importance of various 'special' and para-military forces for maintaining Assad in power. Even less well-known is that since early 2013, and under increasing Iranian influence, these armed forces underwent a gradual transformation into a conglomerate of armed militias, largely consisting of Alawites, members of various intelligence services and Sunni members of the Ba'ath Party.

BACKGROUND OF SYRIAN CONVENTIONAL MILITARY

The Arab Republic of Syria's armed forces can trace their origins to the gendarmerie created by the French Mandate authorities after the conquest of the Kingdom of Syria. Consisting of French officers and native volunteers, in 1925 this force was expanded through the establishment of the Special Troops of the Levant, which saw a limited combat service during the British and Free French invasion of Syria in 1941. French officers remained dominant during the years immediately prior to Syrian independence, but were gradually replaced by Syrian officers educated at the Homs Military Academy and various other institutions in Syria and abroad, before the last of the French left in April 1946. By 1948 the armed forces – which celebrate their

Bashar al-Assad with members of the Syrian General Staff praying at the Tomb of the Unknown Soldier, on the western side of Mount Qasioun, in October 2012. (SANA)

official day of establishment on 1 August – grew to about 12,000 officers and other ranks, which included the Syrian Arab Army, Syrian Arab Air Force and a small Syrian Arab Navy. After the 1948 Arab-Israeli War, the military became heavily involved in politics and it was only after Assad's ascent to power in 1970 that its full attention was again redirected to outside threats.

After being beaten back in a near-defeat while trying to recover the Golan Heights during the October 1973 war, the Syrian military was involved in the civil war in Lebanon in 1976, initially intervening on the side of the Lebanese government against a rebellion of the Palestinian Liberation Organisation (PLO) and various other armed groups. Although badly beaten during the Israeli invasion of Lebanon in June 1982, the Syrian military remained in the country, forging close links to the Iranians who were supporting the establishment of Hezbollah in the mid-1980s. During the latter period, the Syrian armed forces experienced their last major expansion while Hafez al-Assad was attempting to – with extensive support from the Soviet Union – establish a strategic military balance with Israel. This effort eventually failed because the Syrian economy could not support it, but also because Moscow stopped providing arms on favourable conditions. Soviet-Syrian military co-operation practically ceased due to disagreements over resulting debts in 1989. Nevertheless, the defeat of one of the Lebanese armed militias by the Syrian military was instrumental in the ending of the Lebanese civil war in 1990, and Syrian troops remained based in Lebanon until 2005, when they were withdrawn amid public protest and international pressure.

During the 1990s, the general condition of the Syrian military deteriorated dramatically. The collapse of the Soviet Union, break in military relations with Moscow and Russian demands for payments in hard currency resulted in significant problems with re-supply of spares and new equipment. Furthermore, nearly all of the equipment – most of which was based on technologies from the late 1960s and early 1970s, and was unable to match that of the Israeli military – became obsolescent. Combined with the lack of funding, this resulted in most heavy equipment being put into storage.

Things changed to some degree from 1998, when Major General Ali Aslan was appointed Chief of Staff of Armed Forces. A friend of Hafez al-Assad since 1962, Aslan modernised parts of the military through an influx of modern equipment, helped by arms deals that he negotiated around the world, including with Armenia, China, Iran and North Korea. Furthermore, while Syrian military commanders had previously been drilled to lack initiative and refer to superiors in the chain of command for all important decisions, Aslan introduced a new style of military command, encouraging officers to act independently and delegate command, also studying how the Israeli military operated. However, Aslan was unable to find a solution for persistent quarrels with Moscow over debts for equipment delivered in the 1980s, which Damascus continually refused to pay. Therefore, and despite strenuous efforts by the Russians, Syria did not purchase any quantity of modern armament from Moscow before Aslan was forced into retirement in 2002 over differences with Maj Gen Assef Shawkat.

Shawkat's emergence is a classic example of the presence of extended family networks in Assad's control over the Syrian military and security services. During the 1980s and 1990s, many

Maher al-Assad, who underwent 'special forces' training, was officially the commander of the 42nd Armoured Brigade of the 4th Armoured Division in 2011, but according to many sources he was in the position to exercise command over any unit of his preference and was heavily involved in the crackdown on early protests in Syria.
(via Albert Grandolini)

Sand-coloured T-72AVs, like this example photographed in Rif Dimashq in October 2012, are operated by mechanised brigades of the Republican Guards Division – the de-facto private Army of the Syrian government and the strongest unit of the former Syrian military.
(via M.Z.)

members of the al-Assad family began to pursue military careers. One of Hafez al-Assad's first cousins, Maj Gen Shafiq Fayyad (whose son married a daughter of Rifa'at al-Assad), commanded the 3rd Armoured Division in the late 1970s and through the early 1980s. Designated as his original successor, Hafez's oldest son, Bassel al-Assad, went into the Army and became a paratroop-commando in the late 1980s. Maher al-Assad was trained as a special forces operative, and then joined the Republican Guards, where Mustafa Tlass' son Manaf was also to serve until 2011. Bashar initially pursued a civilian career, but after Bassel's death he was recalled to Syria and underwent training at the Military Academy in Homs. One of Bashar's closest friends – and husband of Bashar's sister, Bushra – was Assef Shawkat, who emerged as the strong-man of Syria behind the scenes from 2000, despite a history of sometimes fierce clashes with Maher, and – not being a notable Alawite – having no power base of his own. Shawkat was appointed the Chief of Military Intelligence in 2005.

Meanwhile, since the early summer of 2001, the Syrians had became involved in a 'shadow war' with Israel. This low-intensity conflict was characterised by regular operations of Israeli Defence Force/Air Force (IDF/AF, reorganised as the Israeli Air and Space Force, IASF, in 2005) reconnaissance aircraft and unmanned aerial vehicles (UAVs) over Lebanon and inside Syrian airspace. Most of these operations were undertaken to track deliveries of weapons from Iran and elsewhere to the Syrian military, but especially from and via Syria to Hezbollah in Lebanon. The SyAAF was regularly scrambling its MiG-23s, MiG-25s, and MiG-29s in response, shooting down several Israeli UAVs. In other cases Israeli operations resulted in confrontations with Syrian interceptors, several of which are said to have ended with exchanges of fire – but none were ever confirmed by any official sources.[4]

SPECIAL FORCES AND UNITS WITH SPECIAL PURPOSE

Ever since the establishment of the 1st Parachute Battalion, in 1958, the Syrian military had introduced the long tradition of operating – and then heavily relying upon – special forces (SF) units. By October 1973, the Special Forces Command of the Army – commanded by Maj Gen Ali Haydar – operated nearly two dozen battalions described as 'special forces' (rather resembling Rangers or elite light infantry by their training and capabilities), the most prominent of which became the 82nd Para-Commando that successfully captured the Israeli observation post on Mount Jebel Sheikh.

During subsequent years, the SyAA established 11 SF regiments, four of which were permanently deployed along the Golan Heights. Six other regiments were deployed around sensitive parts of Syria, while a seventh – known only as-Saiqa – became a crack counter-terrorist asset trained in a whole range of special operations, including anti-hijacking and hostage rescue, intelligence gathering and long-range operations beyond enemy lines. Syrian Saiqas are known to have undertaken a number of operations in Lebanon and Jordan in the 1980s and 1990s, but also in the West Bank and – posing as its Druze or Circasian residents – inside Israel too.

The insurgencies of the 1970s and Syrian involvement in the Lebanon war strongly influenced the subsequent development of 'special forces'. Additional units were not only established by regular military branches and intelligence agencies, but were practically independent armed forces: private armies with a separate – almost exclusively Alawist – composition and leadership and only nominal subordination to the Ministry of Defence. For example, by 1982 Rifa'at al-Assad bolstered the SADs to nearly 60,000, organised into 12 armour and artillery brigades, but mostly into light infantry brigades declared 'special forces' because of the 'special' nature of their purpose, training, equipment and pay.

Crucial in the further development of the Syrian military's 'special' assets was November 1983 when, following Hafez's heart problems, Rifa'at attempted to establish himself in power. Rifa'at's coup attempt was spoiled by the quick reaction of the 1st and 3rd Armoured Divisions and Ali Haydar's Special Forces Command, which blocked the SADs while they were deploying into Damascus. While none other than the al-Assad matriarch, Naissa, mediated between her sons to reach a solution by which Rifa'at was sent into exile in France, the SAD was subsequently disbanded. Some of its units were reorganised as the 569th Armoured Division, later reflagged to become the 4th Armoured Division, but the majority were re-assigned to the Republican Guards Division (RGD) and the Army's SF units. In turn, the RGD – which came into being in 1976 as a 15,000-strong armoured division under the command of Adnan Makhouf, first cousin of Hafez al-Assad's wife – was reorganised to consist of three mechanised brigades and two SF security regiments, with particularly strong artillery and air-defence support. While the RGD was stationed in bases on the western side of Mount Qasioun, surrounding the new Presidential Palace, the 4th AD was garrisoned inside a huge military complex in the southern suburbs of Damascus: this ensured that both units were in perfect position to react to any kind of threat for the government.

A fate similar to that of the SAD befell the Army's Special Forces Command in the mid-1990s, when Ali Haydar objected to the possibility of Hafez's succession through Bashar. The general was arrested and his command split into the 14th and 15th Special Forces Division, each subordinated to a different Army corps.

Despite their periodic downfalls, even disbandment, all of the above-mentioned units tended to be better motivated, trained, equipped, paid and more professional than any comparative outfits of the regular Army. They not only bore the brunt of the counter-insurgency effort against the Moslem Brothers and other Sunni groups through the early 1980s, but also fought most important battles in Lebanon during the same period. Furthermore, all were only nominally subordinated to the Chief of Staff of the Syrian Armed Forces – from 2011, Lt Gen Hassan Turkmani: their commanders were responsible directly to the President.

SYRIAN ARAB ARMY

In contrast to the special forces, the Army remained primarily oriented towards defence from outside threats, primarily that from Israel. During the 1980s, the SyAA was expanded and reorganised to consist of three Corps Headquarters (HQ) and 13 conventional armoured and mechanised divisions, most of which consisted of four manoeuvre brigades. The purpose of the 1st Corps was defence against an Israeli invasion over the Golan Heights or through Jordan. It had its units deployed within overlapping positions along two lines of defence (each divided into a northern and southern sector) down the ceasefire lines with Israel and the border to Jordan. As well as exercising control over three mechanised and one armoured divisions, it had one special forces division and two independent infantry brigades under its command. The 2nd Corps was originally responsible for Syrian troops deployed in Lebanon. Following Syrian withdrawal from that country, it became responsible for providing a strategic reserve for the 1st Corps and protecting the border with Lebanon. Correspondingly, it consisted of only two armoured divisions. The 3rd Corps was established with the task of defending the borders to Iraq and Turkey, as well as reinforcing the front in event of a war with Israel. It controlled two armoured divisions and supervised two nominally independent divisions responsible for the defence of northern and eastern Syria. Notably, despite the introduction of the Corps command structure, most division commanders continued reporting directly to the President. Correspondingly, not only the Chief of Staff of the Syrian Armed Forces but also the Corps HQ exercised only a limited operational control over the Army's divisions.

Further down the chain of command, each armoured division was organised into three armoured and one mechanised brigades, usually equipped with Soviet-made T-72 or T-62M main battle tanks (MBTs) and BMP-1 infantry fighting vehicles (IFVs). Mechanised divisions usually consisted of two or three mechanised- and one armoured brigades equipped with Soviet-made T-55 MBTs and BMP-1s. Each division also consisted of combat support elements and a 1,500-strong divisional artillery regiment (divided into three battalions), and at full strength totalled around 15,000 officers and other ranks.

Despite the existence of corps commands and divisions, the primary manoeuvre unit of the SyAA remained brigades, usually made up of between 2,500 and 3,500 soldiers, organised – depending on the type of formation – into either three armoured and one mechanised battalions, or three mechanised and one armoured battalions. Each brigade had its organic air defence, engineering and other combat support elements. Based on these figures, usual assessments cite the SyAA as comprising 220,000 personnel as of 2011, when their nominal organisation was as provided in Table 1.

Actual strength, though, was significantly lower because – while usually commanded by Alawites – most units consisted of Sunni conscripts of dubious loyalty. Furthermore, because lack of funding forced the Army to store much of its heavy equipment, many brigades were maintained at cadre level only. When ordered to mobilise, in March 2011, the ground forces proved unable to bring a majority of their units into operational condition. Out of some 80 brigades of the SyAA, only elements of about 15 ever appeared on the battlefield. Although much under-reported and underestimated, defections and refusals to mobilise were widespread and included the most prestigious units loyal to the government: while between 1,500 and 2,000 officers were arrested, about 100,000 military personnel defected, while a similar number refused to follow calls for mobilisation. Even the RGD and the 4th AD have lost hundreds of officers and other ranks to defections, summary executions, arrests and detention of those suspected of disloyalty. Most SF forces lost nearly 50 percent of their nominal strength. The situation in the remaining conventional Army units was much worse: those that did appear usually only consisted of cadre personnel bunched together from several brigades of the same division, and no 'operational' brigades ever reached even 50 percent of their nominal strength. Correspondingly, the government never managed to bring more than 60,000 troops into operations. Ultimately, combined with the re-assignment of various units to detachments from 'special' units, and extensive combat losses, the scale and impact of desertions resulted in a situation where, by mid-2013, the SyAA practically ceased to exist and its remaining elements were integrated into the NDF and other newly-emerging assets.

MAJOR WEAPONS SYSTEMS

Syrian armed forces were almost exclusively equipped with armament of Soviet origin. Between the mid-1950s and late 1990s, Syria purchased about 4,807 main battle tanks and light tanks, around 3,950 armoured personnel carriers (APCs), infantry fighting vehicles and armoured reconnaissance cars, over 4,000 artillery pieces and 500 multiple rocket launchers. Following often heavy losses in wars with Israel in 1967 and 1973, and after nearly 15 years of wars in Lebanon, as well as delivering about 500 tanks to Iran, Lebanon and other nations, the number of available MBTs

A battery of SyAA 2S1 Gvozdika self-propelled howitzers of 122mm calibre during an exercise in December 2011. At the time this type was operated exclusively by the RGD, 4th AD and armoured formations of the SyAA. (Syrian Ministry of Defence)

Large numbers of obsolete, but significantly upgraded T-55 AMVs – like this example photographed in Dera'a in 2012 – formed the mainstay of armoured and mechanised formations of the Syrian Arab Army. Despite advanced ERA (explosive reactive armour) and fire-control systems, their losses were heavy. (via Tom Cooper)

The 112th Air Defence Regiment of the Republican Guards Division appears to be operating all Russian-made Pantsyr S1 air defence systems delivered to Syria so far, including the example seen here. (Syrian Ministry of Defence)

had decreased to around 2,500 by 2011, more than half of which were in storage. Similarly, the number of operational APCs, IFVs and armoured cars decreased to around 2,000.

The most powerful main battle tanks of the Syrian ground forces at the start of the conflict were 124 T-72M1s, armed with a 125mm calibre smooth-bore gun and upgraded by the Italian-made TURMS-T fire-control system, all of which were assigned to armoured brigades of the RGD. Due to the lack of money, similar modifications were not available for about 500 T-72AVs (equipped with explosive-reactive armour, or ERA), the majority of which were concentrated in the 4th AD, but also the 1st and 3rd ADs.[5] Other armoured divisions were equipped with about 900 older T-72s and T-72Ms – about 100 of which were upgraded to T-72M1M standard with the help of kits purchased from Russia in recent years. At least some armoured formations were still equipped with much older T-62Ms, armed with a 115mm calibre main gun. Mechanised infantry formations were equipped with around 1,000 T-55s (primarily of Czechoslovak production and including about 200 upgraded to T-55AMV standard with

Ukrainian help), with a 100mm calibre main gun, often with different upgrades imported from North Korea.

The primary IFV of the Army comprised some 1,700 BMP-1s, while the mechanised infantry of the RGD was the only to operate about 100 BMP-2s acquired in the late 1990s. About 500 BRDM armoured cars formed the primary element of reconnaissance companies in each armoured and mechanised brigade, while small numbers of BTR-60, BTR-152 and BTR-50s were also operated.

The RGD and 4th AD each operated a field artillery regiment with 30 2S1 and 2S3 self-propelled artillery pieces of 122mm and 152mm calibre respectively. The RGD also included a reinforced air defence regiment equipped with the only SA-8 SAM system in Syrian service: similar formations of other armoured and mechanised divisions were equipped with older SA-9 and SA-13s. The RGD appears to be in control of the only unit equipped with the very advanced SA-22 Pantsyr SAM system, purchased in 2010 with help from Tehran. Furthermore, each armoured and

Multiple Rocket Launch Systems (MRLS) – like the BM-21 installed on a URAL-475D truck, seen here – represented the main weapon of about a dozen missile and artillery brigades of the SyAA. Many rounds fired by them were manufactured in Egypt and imported in the 1980s and 1990s. (Syrian Ministry of Defence)

Large numbers of Russian-made Gaz-469C 'general-purpose utility vehicles' (Jeeps) are in service with most Syrian military units. (Photo by Alexandar Hunger)

A Jowlan-2 (Scud-B) surface-to-surface missile (imported either from North Korea or Iran) being prepared for launch during an exercise in October 2011. (Syrian Ministry of Defence)

mechanised division included an anti-aircraft regiment equipped with 32 ZSU-23-4 self-propelled anti-aircraft guns (SPAAGs), while a large number of towed anti-aircraft artillery pieces were in storage or used for training.

Except for their usual field artillery regiments equipped with 30 2S1 self-propelled guns of 122mm calibre, armoured and mechanised formations deployed along the Golan Heights were reinforced with additional batteries equipped with towed guns like the D-30 and M-31/37 (122mm calibre), M-54 (152mm calibre) and around 100 T-12 anti-tank guns of 100mm calibre. The same types of towed guns represented the major equipment of artillery formations in other divisions. Furthermore, each brigade of the Syrian Army included a battery of six ZSU-23-4 self-propelled, radar controlled anti-aircraft guns with four barrels (23mm calibre).

The SyAA's infantry formations and dedicated anti-tank formations used to operate huge numbers of guided anti-tank missiles (ATGMs), ranging from older AT-3s and AT-4s to more recent AT-10s and AT-14s (French-made MILAN ATGMs, successfully deployed by Syrians during the wars in Lebanon, were meanwhile withdrawn from service). Significant stocks of man-portable air defence systems (MANPADs) like SA-7s, SA-14s and SA-18s were withdrawn from service and put into deep storage at the start of the conflict, in order to prevent their capture by insurgents.

In regard of infantry weapons, the ubiquitous AK-47 assault rifle remains the primary weapon of the Syrian military, although its more modern variants – including the AK-74M – are used by special forces. Light and general-purpose machine guns are primarily of PKM type, while the DShK heavy machine gun is also in widespread service, in addition to several other types, available in smaller numbers.

The last part of the Syrian ground forces to become involved in the conflict, the Missile Command, used to be headquartered in Aleppo before the war, but is otherwise the least-known element of Syria's armed forces. This force apparently included the 96th Missile Brigade, which used to be equipped with about 90 antiquated FROG-7 surface-to-surface missiles (SSMs). Few such weapons were fired against insurgent-held areas in late 2012, but this unit is meanwhile primarily deploying about 200 Iranian-made Fateh-110 (named Teshreen by Syrians) and Zelzal (named Misseloon in Syria) SSMs imported since the mid-2000s. The most important Syrian unit operating ballistic missiles is the 115th Missile Brigade equipped with – among others – nine 9K72 transporter-erector-launchers (TELs) for SS-1C Scud-Bs and their foreign variants. Syria purchased some 190 R-17E missiles for this system from the former Soviet Union. During the 1990s and 2000s, up to 1,000 Scud-B variants and additional TELs were purchased from North Korea and Iran, under the designations Hwasong-6 and Shahab-3 respectively (Syrians named them Jowlan-2). While the majority of warheads for such weapons were conventional, about 150 were modified for deployment of chemical weapons. Other Missile Brigades – like the 155th and 156th – are equipped with locally-manufactured M-301 and Failaq-2, or BM-21 and BM-27 multiple-rocket systems of Russian origin.[6]

Table 1:
Syrian Ground Forces, Nominal Order of Battle, March 2011

Unit & Main base	HQ/Base	Heavy Equipment (if operated)	Commanders & Deployments
President of the Syrian Arab Republic and Commander in Chief of Armed Forces: Bashar Hafez al-Assad Minister of Defence: Lt Gen Ali Habib Mahmoud (replaced by Lt Gen Abdullah Dawoud Rajiha on 9 Aug 2011, replaced by Lt Gen Fahad al-Jasem el-Freij on 19 Jul 2012) Chief of Staff Syrian Armed Forces: Lt Gen Abdullah Dawoud Rajiha (replaced by Lt Gen Assef Shawkat on 9 Aug 2011) Chief of Staff SyAA: Maj Gen Fahad al-Jasem el-Freij Director of SyAA Security: Maj Gen Bashar Bassam Merhej Commander Military Police: Maj Gen Mohammed Ibrahim Sha'ar (appointed MOI, 14 April 2011) Commander Engineer Corps: Brig Gen Jehad Shehadeh			
Units Reporting directly to the President of Syrian Arab Republic			
Republican Guards Division	Mt Qasioun, Damascus		CO Maj Gen Mohammad Shoaib Ali Suleiman; XO Brig Gen Mohammad Qasim
100th Artillery Regiment		BM-21, BM-30, Failaq-2	operating chemical weapons
101st Security Regiment			
102nd Security Regiment			Nawa 2011
104th Brigade		BMP-2, T-72AV	CO Brig Gen Manaf Tlas; replaced by Brig Gen Essam Zaher el-Din (or Zahreddine); Douma & Harasta 2011; Aleppo 2013; reorganised as 104th Airborne Brigade in 2014
105th Brigade		T-72AV TURMS-T, T-72AV TURMS-T	CO Brig Gen Talal Makhlouf; incl. 17th Battalion; Douma & Harasta 2011; Qalamoun 2013; disbanded in early 2014
106th Brigade		BMP-2, T-72AV	CO Brig Gen Mohammed Khadur Douma & Harasta 2011; Qalamoun 2013
112th Air Defence Regiment		SA-8, Pantsyr S1	Damascus
?? Artillery Regiment		2S1, 2S3	
4th Armoured Division			CO Maj Gen Mohammed Ali Durgham replaced by Maj Gen Ali Ammar, November 2011
40th Armoured Brigade		T-72AV, BMP-1	Damascus 2011
41st Armoured Brigade		T-72AV, BMP-1	CO Brig Gen Ali Ammar (appointed CO 4th AD in November 2011); Damascus & Homs 2011
42nd Armoured Brigade		T-72AV, BMP-1	CO Brig Gen Maher al-Assad XO Brig Gen Jawdat Ibrahim Safi; incl. 154th Regiment; Moadamiya, Douma, Dmeyr 2011
138th Mechanised Brigade		BMP-1, T-72AV	Banias & Homs 2011; part defected in January 2012 while deployed near Sheikh Miskin and Saida
555th Airborne Regiment			CO Brig Gen Jamal Yunes; Moadamiya, Darayya, Jisr ash-Shugur 2011; Homs 2012; Qalamoun 2013

154th Artillery Regiment		2S1, 2S3	reorganised as '154th Brigade NDF', 2014
SF Command			CO Maj Gen Ahmad al-Fri, replaced by Maj Gen Bader Aqel XO Maj Gen Fouad Hamoudeh
41st SF Regiment	el-Dreij		CO Brig Gen Adnan Deeb (KIA November 2011) Dera'a & Homs 2011
45th SF Regiment			CO Brig Gen Ghassan Afif; incl. 230th & 625th SF Battalion; Banias, Bayda & Homs 2011
46th SF Regiment			Idlib & Hama 2011; overrun at Atareb (Base 46) Idlib, November 2012
47th SF Regiment	el-Dreij		incl. 62nd Battalion; Dera'a and Hama 2011; Idlib 2012
53rd SF Regiment			CO Brig Gen George Solomon Banias & Qalat Markab 2011; Homs 2012
54th SF Regiment			CO Brig Gen Aladdin Rajab Homs 2012 then Hassakah Province
416th SF Regiment	Tartous		established 2012 in Tartous as NDF unit; deployed in Aleppo ever since
14th SF Division			CO Maj Gen Hussein
35th SF Regiment			CO Brig Gen Ramadan Mahmoud Ramadan; Dera'a & Banias 2011; Homs & Idlib 2012
36th SF Regiment			Homs 2012
554th SF Regiment			Homs 2012
556th SF Regiment			Homs 2012
15th SF Division	**as-Suwayda**		CO Maj Gen Ghassan
37th SF Regiment			cadre only; Homs 2012
127th SF Regiment			incl. 3rd SF Battalion; Dera'a 2011; Homs 2012
404th Armoured Regiment		T-55	Homs 2012
405th Artillery Regiment			
I Corps, HQ Damascus **CO Maj Gen Faraq Shehada (POW 29 June 2012)**			
5th Mechanised Division	**az-Zadi**		CO Maj Gen Suheil Salman Hassan XO Brig Gen Ali Badi
35th Mechanised Brigade		BMP-1, T-55	cadre only
112th Mechanised Brigade	Isra	BMP-1, T-55	28th and 171st Battalion mobilised; Bosra & Nawa 2011
132nd Mechanised Brigade	Dera'a	BMP-1, T-55	CO Brig Gen Ahmed Yousef Jarad; 59th Battalion (to al-Herak) and 287th Battalion (to Dera'a), 2011
12th Armoured Brigade	Isra	T-55, BMP-1	CO Brig Gen Mohsin Makhlouf; cadre deployed at al-Herak 2011
175th Artillery Regiment	Isra	2S1	cadre only; never deployed outside base; overrun in February 2014
691st MP Battalion			Dera'a 2011
7th Mechanised Division			
68th Mechanised Brigade	Husseniye	BMP-1, T-55	parts defected in Hama, 2011; battalion to Zabadani 2011-2012, cadre and base overrun in December 2013
88th Mechanised Brigade	Andan	BMP-1, T-55	cadre only, base overrun and most of T-55s captured, July/August 2012
121st Mechanised Brigade	'Kanacker'	BMP-1, T-55	CO Brig Gen Ghanim (KIA 4 November 2011); Damascus 2011-2012
78th Armoured Brigade		T-55, BMP-1	cadre used to form a battalion-sized TF including remnants of 88th and 121st Brigades; Damascus 2011; Aleppo, 2012
85th Artillery Regiment			
9th Armoured Division			CO Maj Gen Yusuf Ahmed
33rd Armoured Brigade	Misimiya	T-72, BMP-1	incl. 42nd, 43rd and 44th Tank Battalions, and 46th Mechanised Battalion; cadre mobilised only; never deployed outside base
34th Armoured Brigade	Halfaya (Hama)	T-72, BMP-1	incl. 51st and 52nd Battalions; cadre mobilised only; never deployed outside base; overrun December 2012
43rd Armoured Brigade		T-72, BMP-1	
52nd Mechanised Brigade		BMP-1, T-72	as-Suwayda & Horan, 2011; hit by defections following deployment to al-Herak, August 2011; disbanded

15th Artillery Regiment	Sanamein	2S1	
61st Infantry Brigade (Independent)	Tel al-Jabiyeh/ Nawa		Base overrun by insurgents in February 2014
90th Infantry Brigade (Independent)	Quneitra		Base overrun by insurgents in February 2014

II Corps, HQ Zabadani

1st Armoured Division	**Kisweh, Rif Dimashq**		CO Maj Gen Yusuf al-Assad
76th Armoured Brigade		T-72, BMP-1	cadre reinforced by elements of other brigades; reorganised as Death Brigade NDF
91st Armoured Brigade		T-72, BMP-1	cadre assigned to 76th Brigade
153rd Armoured Brigade		T-72, BMP-1	cadre assigned to 76th Brigade
58th Mechanised Brigade		BMP-1, T-72	Rif Dimashq 2011-2013
216th Artillery Regiment		2S1, 2S3	
10th Armoured Division	**Homs**		
56th Armoured Brigade		T-72, BMP-1	Zabadani 2011; in Azzaz, Minakh AB and Aleppo since 2012
18th Mechanised Brigade		BMP-1, T-72	cadre assigned to 56th Brigade
62nd Mechanised Brigade		BMP-1, T-72	reorganised as a small TF in January 2012, under Col Fawaz Hassan; active in Idlib and Lattakia until November 2012; to NDF in 2013
85th Mechanised Brigade	Aleppo	BMP-1, T-72	cadre mobilised; Aleppo & Jisr ash-Shugur 2011; Aleppo 2012; to NDF in 2013
?? Artillery Regiment			
15th Infantry Brigade (Independent)	Homs		one battalion mobilised in late 2011; parts related to a tribe from Dayr az-Zawr defected in spring 2012

III Corps, Aleppo

3rd Armoured Division	**Qutayfah & Dmeyr**		CO Maj Gen Naim Jassem Suleiman; division transferred from III Corps to C-in-C Armed Forces in November 2011; reorganised as 3rd Infantry Division NDF in early 2014
47th Armoured Brigade	an-Nasiriyah	T-72, BMP-1	Battalion to Hama 2011-2013; cadre and base of 555th Battalion overrun in October 2013
65th Armoured Brigade		T-72, BMP-1	CO Brig Gen Jihad Mohammed Sultan Dera'a & Douma 2011; Homs 2012; Qalamoun 2013
81st Armoured Brigade	ar-Ruhaiba	T-72, BMP-1	four companies mobilised; Zabadani & Dera'a 2011; base overrun late 2013
21st Mechanised Brigade		BMP-1, T-72	128th Battalion mobilised; Qalamoun 2012-2013
123rd Artillery Regiment		2S1	in Hassakah since 2012
67th Artillery Regiment		D-30, M54	two battalions mobilised, to NDF in 2013 then to Qalamoun
11th Armoured Division	**Hama**		CO Maj Gen Mohammad Deeb Zaitoun; XO Brig Gen Mou'az Waakad Abu Assaaf (KIA 2014) elements mobilised and deployed to Hama, 2011; large part surrounded and besieged at Wadi ad-Dayf base, in 2012; destroyed during withdrawal from Wadi ad-Dayf, late 2014
60th Armoured Brigade		T-62M, BMP-1	ar-Rastan 2011; parts of unit defected
67th Armoured Brigade		T-62M, BMP-1	Homs, 2011; parts of unit defected; Qalamoun 2013
?? Armoured Brigade		T-62M, BMP-1	status unclear
87th Mechanised Brigade		BMP-1, T-62M	Hama 2011-2013
89th Artillery Regiment			
17th Mechanised Division	**Dayr az-Zawr**		
110th Mechanised Brigade		BMP-1, T-55	deployed Lattakia October-November 2011, but large parts defected
133rd Mechanised Brigade		BMP-1, T-55	two battalions combined with artillery regiment securing Dayr az-Zawr AB
137th Mechanised Brigade		BMP-1, T-55	119th and 240th Battalion mobilised; largely defected or destroyed in Dayr az-Zawr 2011-2012
93rd Armoured Brigade		T-55, BMP-1	Idlib 2011; ar-Raqqa 2012; ar-Rastan 2012-2013
64th Artillery Regiment			
18th Armoured Division	**Aleppo**		

131st Armoured Brigade		T-55, BMP-1	
134th Armoured Brigade		T-55, BMP-1	CO Brig Gen Yousef Ismail; 990th Battalion mobilised (CO Col For'ad Khaddour), ar-Rastan & Talbiseh 2011; Eastern Ghouta & Qalamoun 2013
167th Armoured Brigade		T-55, BMP-1	CO Brig Gen Ali Mohamed Hamdan; 324th Battalion mobilised; ar-Rastan 2011;
120th Mechanised Brigade		BMP-1, T-55	ar-Rastan 2011-2012; to NDF 2013
80th Air Defence Regiment		ZSU-23-4	cadre mobilised for protection of base and Nayrab AB/Aleppo IAP
135th Artillery Regiment		D-30, M-54	incl. 23rd Artillery Battalion; cadre mobilised only; overrun by insurgents in December 2012
Coastal Guard Brigade	Lattakia	4 TELs for SS-C-1B Sepal, 6 TELs for SS-C-3 Styx; partially replaced by K-300P Bastion (with S-800 Yakonth/SS-N-26 missiles since November 2011)	incl. missile battalions in Lattakia, Banias, Hamidiyeh and Tartous; 157th Coastal Guard Battalion (motorised infantry formation); and a battalion of PT-76 light tanks

INTELLIGENCE APPARATUS

Over the last 40 years, the government of Syria has established a decentralised network of about 20 security agencies with overlapping responsibilities. The primary purpose of them all was to control the military and population and maintain the government in power, though in recent years some of these were also yielding additional income for the government. Large parts of this network functioned as an extensive system of personal relationships and patronage, usually based on family connections. It is because of mutual interests that this system proved highly resistant to the insurgency.

Nominally, the work of all intelligence agencies is overseen by the National Security Bureau (commanded by Lt Gen Hisham Bakhtiyar). In practice, major intelligence services are acting as autonomous entities that report directly to the President. The following overview considers only services known to have operated their own armed units or to have closely co-operated with various military services and para-military organisations (described further below) since 2011.

The most powerful and notorious intelligence service in Syria since the late 1960s – and one of the main instigators of repression against any kind of opposition – was the Air Force Intelligence Directorate (Idarat al-Mukhabarat al-Jawiyya, AFI). Reorganised from a relatively minor security service responsible for control of the SyAAF in the 1960s – and hardly ever busy collecting intelligence related to its official title – the AFI became involved in suppression of protest from their start. Commanded by Maj Gen Jamil Hassan, it operates through its Investigative Branch (CO Brig Gen Abdul Salem Fajer Mahmoud) and Special Operations Branch (CO Col Ghassan Ismail), each of which run a large number of cells all over the country. Reports from people who were detained by the AFI indicate that the Investigative Branch is in charge of three detention facilities, the biggest of which is at Almazza AB, which is also the HQ of this service. The AFI should also have been in control of Syrian chemical weapons, which in turn were usually deployed by the 100th Artillery Regiment of the RGD.

Although there are reports that the AFI was responsible for certain operations outside Syria, it seems that such were rather within the responsibility of the Military Intelligence Directorate or Department of Military Intelligence (Shu'bat al-Mukhabarat al-Askariyya, SMA). Originally established during the French Mandate period as the Deuxiéme Bureau and headquartered at Sassa, in southern Damascus, the SMA operates from offices in Aleppo, Idlib, Homs and Hama, and closely co-operates with various special forces assets. As far as is known, the SMA is commanded by Maj Gen Abdul Fatah Kudsiyeh. It consists of the Military Investigative Branch, Palestine Investigative Branch, Communications Security and Surveillance Branch and several Security Branches – essentially field units deployed to control the function of different military units – deployed in specific regions. Further down its chain of command, the SMA is known to include departments like Military Interrogation, the Raid Branch (Unit 235), Military Security Branch, Wireless Branch (Unit 293, also responsible for internet security), Foreign Section (Unit 279), Palestine Section (Unit 237), but foremost of all the Internal Affairs Branch (Unit 293), with several branches in Damascus (Units 215, 235, and 291, for example), Idlib (Unit 271), Dera'a (Unit 245) and others. Commanded by former chief of the AFI, Maj Gen Abdel-Fatah Qudsiyeh, until 2012, and by Maj Gen Rafiq Shahadah ever since, the SMA closely co-operates with the Army's SF assets.

Also headquartered at Sassa is the General Intelligence (or Security) Directorate (Idarat al-Amn al-Amn, or SSI), often referred to by its old name, State Security. Although including an External Security Division responsible for foreign intelligence work (Unit 300), the SSI is primarily responsible for the surveillance of the Syrian population. Organised into Espionage (Unit 251), Information Security (Unit 255) and Investigative Branches (Unit 285), the SSI also includes the Raid Branch that operates a number of raid squadrons – units responsible for tracking down, arresting and executing political opponents – in all major Syrian cities. Said to have been commanded by Brig Gen Hisham Bakhtiar (or Ikhtiyar) – supposedly a Shi'a of Iranian origin and close friend of Bashar al-Assad and Assef Shawkat – in the period 2001–2005, the SSI was under the command of Brig Gen Zohair Hamad from 2010 until July 2012, and Brig Gen Mohammad Dib Zaitoun ever since.

The Political Security Directorate (Idarat al-Amn al-Siyasi, PSD) is responsible for monitoring political dissent, the media and all registered political parties and for running state prisons. Commanded by Brig Gen Zaitoun until 2012, it has since been run by Brig Gen Rustum Ghazali, and is known to have been actively involved in the prosecution, detention, torture and

Another type of 'commercial enterprise' run on behalf of officials from various Syrian intelligence agencies, and in co-operation with para-military and criminal networks better known as 'Shabiha', was the 'import and export' of Jihadists from around the world into Iraq during the 2000s. For this purpose, one of Syria's intelligence officers – Abu el-Kaka, seen on these two photos – became prominent while acting as an Islamist preacher who was calling 'volunteers' to go to Iraq and fight the USA. (via Tom Cooper)

Members of the Shabiha proudly displaying their muscles with Assad tattoos. Usually recruited for their physical strength, lack of education and blind loyalty to the Alawite sect and the Assad family in particular, since the start of the conflict in Syria they have become ever more important for ensuring the survival of the government. (via Tom Cooper)

During the late 1990s, Syria became a major hub for arms trafficking between Iran and the Hezbollah in Lebanon, but also from different sources in Eastern Europe to various destinations in Africa. It was during this time that anonymous transport aircraft of Soviet/Russian origin – like this Antonov An-12 – became a common sight even at Damascus IAP. (Photo by Tom Cooper)

murder of dozens of thousands of members of the opposition.

Overall, large parts of these – and other – security agencies began to act like pro-government militias right from the start of the uprising. Relying on a widespread network of informers, they might have boasted up to 200,000 personnel by late 2011. Their militias were regularly deployed as infantry right behind SyAA formations, carefully monitoring their movement and operations, and – for example – summarily executing soldiers who refused to open fire at protesters. Since 2013, such militias began supplanting detachments from overstretched loyalist units like the 4th AD and various SF regiments in being deployed to directly corset former SyAA units and some of the below-mentioned para-military deemed less reliable. Eventually, because of the de-facto demise of the former Army and increasing importance of para-military groups, most such militias were integrated into para-military organisations in 2013.

PARA-MILITARY ORGANISATIONS: SHABIHA, BA'ATH PARTY MILITIA AND POPULAR COMMITTEES

Originally the lowest level in the network, consisting of units with special purpose, regular military forces and intelligence services, various para-military organisations have been playing an important role in the control of the Syrian population since the 1970s. Indeed, since the start of unrest in 2011, even para-military organisations that were never effectively controlled by the government are fighting for it because of their beliefs and personal loyalties. Generally known as 'Shabiha' (Ghosts) within the Syrian population, three major Alawite-dominated para-military organisations came into being over time. While usually not distinguished from each other by the opposition or in media reports, they meanwhile represent some of most important combat assets of the government. Lacking enough reliable military forces to control all of the country, but in position to still rely on a hard core of supporters among a significant portion of the population, the government gradually melded most of what was left of the former Syrian Arab Army with several different para-miltiary groups.

Shabiha is actually Syrian slang used to describe a specific class of Alawite smugglers from the Lattakia area in the 1970s and 1980s. It came into being from the car preferred by them, the Mercedes Shabah, or Ghost. Ironically, this mafia-like criminal network was originally run by nobody else but members of the extended Assad family, the most famous of whom were Fawaza and Mudhir al-Assad, nephews of Hafez al-Assad. While traditionally profiting from their activities and tolerating them, the government never

Members of one of the militias run by the Ministry of Interior, as seen in 2013. Most such units have meanwhile been integrated into the National Defence Force (NDF). (Photo by Shady Hulwe)

really controlled them. On the other hand, the average Shabiha was usually selected for his physical strength, lack of education and blind loyalty to the Alawite sect and the Assad family in particular. Correspondingly, and despite their history of insubordination, as soon as the protests began, they sided with the government.

Early on, the Shabiha militants were usually deployed separately from regular armed forces and intelligence services. They would mingle amongst the protesters, sow chaos and carry out acts of violence, enabling the government to challenge the legitimacy of the protesters. Since summer 2011, they began appearing with intelligence operatives, and sometimes monitored them too, and then started donning military-like uniforms and intimidating the population. As the conflict progressed, the Shabiha received more important roles, including protection of security facilities and prisons, and even interrogation of those in opposition. Ironically, since the start of the Civil War, many of them became rich through selling arms to insurgents.

The original organisational structure of the Shabiha remains unknown, while their strength in numbers was usually estimated at between 5,000 and 10,000 – each paid up to US$40 a day. Many additional Shabihas were subsequently recruited, trained by Iranian instructors and organised into small units concentrated primarily in regions known as loyal to the government, like Qardaha, Jabla, Tartous and Lattakia.

Additional similar militias from members of other ethnic groups have been created since late 2012. Among these is the Sunni Berri family from Aleppo (known for its involvement in drugs and arms smuggling) and a similar Sunni network in Dayr az-Zawr, but also a large number of criminals released from prisons in exchange for loyalty to the regime.

Quantitatively, the biggest Syrian para-military force was established following the January 1980 Ba'ath Party Congress, when the government began to arm and train thousands of supporters throughout the country. Leading members of the Ba'ath Partry were encouraged to stockpile arms and ammunition in case of emergency. It was in this fashion that Popular Organisations came into being, also known as the People's Army (Jaysh ash-Sha'abi) or the Ba'ath Party Militia (Munazzamat Sha'biya, BPM). One might wonder about Bashar al-Assad's decision to depend upon the Ba'ath Party for support, considering this had some two million members around the country and included many non-Alawites. However, except for a relatively small number of members from Dera'a Province that defected early after the siege of Dera'a in spring 2011, the majority of the party remained loyal. Obviously they are not keen to experience any kind of political competition that could undermine the Ba'ath Party's monopoly on power.

By 2011, the BPM was estimated to be able to put as many as 100,000 paramilitaries under arms, mostly Shi'a, Druze and Christians, but a few Alawites too. According to Iranian sources, since 2012 the BPM has been re-modelled after the Basij Corps of the Islamic Revolutionary Guards (IRGC) of Iran, and about 50,000 of its combatants underwent training courses run with Iranian support. By 2013, they had become crucially important for the survival of a number of government garrisons in Aleppo and Hama provinces.

Primarily staffed by minority populations, who organised and armed themselves to protect their towns and neighbourhoods from insurgents, are the Popular Committees (Lijan Sha'biya). The first of these were raised from Alawite, Christian and Druze communities in the 1980s, although many of them came into being out of a desire for self-protection and less because of support for the government. Others formed because many in the Alawite community fear that they will be punished for the government's atrocities over the past 40 years, regardless of being involved or supporting them or not. Nevertheless, most have subsequently received weapons from the government and a hand-picked selection from the Damascus area was organised into some 20,000-strong Struggle Companies (Saraya al-Syra), commanded by Adnan al-Assad.

While originally manning a large number of check-points at entrances to nearly every village or minor town that remained under government control, they have meanwhile been re-trained and re-organised to receive a much more important role. Namely, upon Iranian insistence and out of necessity to replace heavy losses it suffered in 2012, since early 2013 the government has taken steps to formalise and professionalise the Popular Committee militias. Through a combination of many scattered detachments from the former SyAA, raid squadrons of different intelligence agencies and various Shabiha gangs, the Iranian officers subsequently created the National Defence Forces (Quwwat ad-Difa'a al-Watani, NDF).

3
MASSACRES OF PROTESTERS

Organising protests against the tyranny and perversion of a government as entrenched as that in Damascus was by no means an easy choice for Syrian activists, but it seems that many of them had no idea that Assad would react in the most brutal fashion imaginable. However, in the light of all the problems the country was facing, and government manipulation of inner politics and media, there was practically no other option. Early calls for protests issued via social media in mid-February 2011 had failed to attract much attention. Before long, some foreign commentators rushed to explain that Syria was a different case than Tunisia, Egypt or Libya – where mass protesting erupted around the same time. Supposedly, Bashar al-Assad had not only 'built a sturdy house', but was also popular and then strengthened by the collapse of pro-Western governments in Egypt and Tunisia.[7]

Actually, the roots of Syrian protesting were to be found within an entirely new generation of young, apolitical and secular Syrians, including not only Sunnis but other ethnic, tribal and religious groups too, who had no affiliations with older political ideologies or connections to Syrian political emigrants living abroad. While they took their time to organise, this gap between secular activists in Syria and the politically and/or religiously-motivated opposition abroad was to come as a surprise for many foreign observers: very few activists involved in organising mass protests paid attention to oppositionals abroad. Therefore, most early attempts by Syrians in diaspora to exercise influence upon the revolution failed. It was only later that this gap was to prove one of the major hindrances for the evolution of not only the protest movement, but also the subsequent uprising and insurgency.

CRADLE OF THE REVOLUTION

As could be expected, the SMA's Unit 293 reacted to internet calls for demonstrations by turning off large parts of the internet network in Syria, while the SSI began searching for and arresting anybody suspected of involvement in protesting. Although tensions rose, the majority of the population remained quiet – for a while.

On 15 March 2011, the streets of Dera'a filled with thousands of protesters who demanded an end to corruption and repression. The AFI and SSI operatives were immediately on the scene and opened fire into the mass, killing the first four victims of the coming war. Protesting continued, nevertheless, and funeral ceremonies for victims of oppression spontaneously turned into mass protesting on 18 March 2011. One peacefully protesting column run into a security checkpoint on the outskirts of the city, where regime forces opened fire: 30 civilians were shot dead and dozens wounded. The next day, more spontaneous popular protests followed – this time against corruption and repression – which gradually turned into riots, as the people began attacking symbols of the government and torched the Ba'ath Party HQ and Syriatel building. The security forces withdrew from the streets to the rooftops, from where they opened fire at unarmed civilians below, and yet more people were killed. Protesting went on into the night, centring around the Omari Mosque in the centre of the city.

The government reacted with lame conciliatory gestures and the discharge of Faysal Ahmad Kalthoum from his post as governor of Dera'a Province. Both were measures for public purposes: actually, Bashar al-Assad wanted to take the protesting offline and finish it through killing, arresting, torturing and murdering protesters. Correspondingly, he ordered his security services to put an end to protesting – within the shortest possible time, and regardless of cost. His order set large parts of the security apparatus into motion. The 41st and 47th SF Regiments based at Camp al-Dreij near Damascus were mobilised and deployed to Dera'a on board SyAAF Mi-8 and Mi-17 helicopters. The 35th SF Regiment arrived from its base in as-Suwayda, followed

A typical peaceful demonstration in the Bab Dreeb neighbourhood of Homs, as staged in thousands of cases all over Syria through 2011 and into the first half of 2012. (via R. S.)

by mechanised companies from the 4th AD, 132nd Mechanised Brigade (5th MD), and the 65th Armoured Brigade (3rd AD), which arrived from their bases in the Damascus area. Operational HQ of this task force – commanded by Brig Gen Ali Abbas Sharif from the 4th AD – was set up at the local football stadium, which was subsequently used as a huge detention camp run by the AFI and SSI.

Intending to apply the same doctrine and tactics that proved so effective in the early 1980s, Sharif launched his assault on 23 March. While deploying mechanised forces to surround Dera'a and isolate it from the outside world, he sent black-clad special forces to assault a huge protest that was gathering around the Omari mosque, shortly after midnight. Although civilians demonstrated peacefully and were not armed, soldiers and operatives opened fire, killing seven, and went on to arrest dozens. When protesters returned to the streets the following morning, special forces launched an assault on the compound of the Omari mosque where several hundred protesters armed with rocks, sticks and knives entrenched themselves. Following four days of repeated attacks, more than 60 civilians were killed inside and hundreds wounded. Many injured protesters brought to local hospitals were subsequently taken away by security forces and disappeared forever. Unable to hide this crisis from the public, the government launched a 'public-relations' campaign, declaring that this assault was in response to a conspiracy instigated from abroad, supposedly aiming to launch an uprising of 'armed Salafists' in Dera'a.

After reinforcing locally-deployed units of special forces, Army and intelligence services to about 6,000 – including much of the 138th Brigade from the 4th AD – the government launched a major military operation to suppress resistance in Dera'a. The deployment of the 138th Brigade was organised in a particularly interesting fashion, which was subsequently applied all around Syria, in turn creating much confusion in related reporting. Namely, a company from this 'loyalist' brigade was assigned to supervise and work with two companies each from the 3rd and 5th Divisions, in turn creating a new, three-company battalion (or 'task force'), run under the flag of the 4th Armoured and the leadership of its commanders.

Dera'a was besieged by 25 April, with the newly-created task force of the 4th AD sealing off major streets and easily smashing through a few improvised, shallow barricades erected by protesters. Water, food, electricity and telecommunications were cut off as the military launched repeated raids, in the course of which dozens were killed and thousands arrested. As protesting continued and then spread into surrounding towns and villages, soldiers were ordered to open fire and 'to kill' – not only any protesters, but whoever they saw on the street, balconies or even rooftops. Commanders and operatives from intelligence services were always standing right behind troops, carefully controlling them to shoot into protesters.

Syrian state-controlled media was quick to start releasing photos and videos from Dera'a, supposedly showing 'gunmen shooting at unarmed civilians and security forces'. Bodies of executed soldiers were always taken away by the AFI and the next day presented by Syrian TV as 'killed by terrorists'. Actually, the gangs in question were members of intelligence agencies dressed in civilian clothes and either shooting at military units in order to provoke them to open fire, or 'punishing' soldiers who refused to follow the order 'to kill'. Dozens of cases are known where – upon identifying soldiers who either did not shoot or fired into the air – commanders of nearby intelligence operatives would call snipers positioned on roofs of surrounding buildings to shoot and kill such soldiers.

Before long, this provoked serious tensions between the Sunni troops of the special forces, the 3rd and 5th Divisions, and the Alawite, Christian and Druze soldiers from the same and other units, especially the 4th AD.[8] After intelligence services reacted with arrests and summary executions of officers and soldiers from the 65th Armoured Brigade, parts of this unit mutinied. Some sided with protesters, while others defected and ran away: one officer took two companies of infantry and two T-55 tanks with him, another sabotaged four T-55s before leaving.[9] On 27 April, some defectors clashed with elements of the 4th AD deployed to control them and there was a short battle in which both sides suffered losses. In a furious action of special forces and the 4th AD, the resistance of defectors was broken and on 28 April the government reinforced its attack on Dera'a, announcing its intention to 'prevent the declaration of a Salafist Emirate in the city'.[10]

A still from a video showing a Syrian Army soldier with arrested protesters in Dera'a, many of whom were either summarily executed or detained by one of the intelligence services, never to be seen again. (via Tom Cooper)

A still from a video showing a BMP-1 of the 5th MD on the streets of Dera'a. Its badly beaten-up and worn-out impression is typical for practically all vehicles of the Syrian military. (via R. S.)

Unaware of the government's intentions, on 29 April villagers from surrounding areas attempted to peacefully break the siege and bring food into the city. Declaring the people marching to Dera'a as 'Islamists coming to kidnap women and children in predominantly Christian areas', the commanders of SF units and the 4th AD set up a trap near the military housing in Saida, a small town 10km east of Dera'a, and ordered their troops to open fire. At least 98, possibly up to 120, civilians were killed in cold blood. On 1 May, Dera'a was for the first time subjected to artillery shelling and even air attacks by several Mi-8s that deployed unguided rockets in attacks on protesters. The city remained under a siege for several months. According to local sources, over 3,000 people were killed in Dera'a between mid-March and mid-July 2011, while thousands are still missing.

While 'mopping up' after the massacre in Saida, on 29 April, AFI operatives arrested about 160 civilians, including a group of children caught while writing anti-Assad messages on the wall surrounding their school in Saida. Making no distinction between adults and adolescents, intelligence operatives severely tortured the children and 13-year-old Hamza al-Khatib was murdered under torture. The return of Hamza's body – clearly showing scars, lacerations, bruises and burns to his feet, elbows, face and knees, consistent with the use of electric shock devices, and with his genitals castrated – to his parents on 29 May was the drop that spilled the barrel. Although most of the unrest in Dera'a was suppressed by that time, publications about his fate sparked a popular revolution.

WAVE OF DEFECTIONS

Protesting in Dera'a spread to Damascus, Homs and Hama, and then to Aleppo, Banias, Dayr az-Zawr, Hassakah, Idlib, Lattakia, Qamishli, Raqqah, Suwayda, and Tartus by 25 March 2011. Tens of thousands of ordinary people marched – first in protest against the government, then in funerals for the dead. Defying the crackdown and widespread, systematic attacks by security forces that killed hundreds, including many children, and arrested nearly 50,000 people, protests continued unabated. Although the majority of detainees were subsequently released, more than 15,000 have disappeared or the government returned only their mutilated bodies to their families. Such methods of terror backfired severely, the torture and killings giving a new impetus to the revolution, prompting ever more protesting. Unsurprisingly, President Assad's offer of 'national dialogue' and various political concessions were understood as hollow promises and brought no respite. His deeds did not follow his words: when murderous attacks by intelligence services, Shabiha and the military made large-scale, mass protesting too dangerous, activists reorganised their operations, staging a huge wave of smaller scale protests by night. Despite a crackdown on mass media, every morning thousands of videos about protesting from thousands of different districts in larger cities, nearly every town and village were uploaded on the internet. By the end of May, all of Syria was in uproar.

Military-wise, the government was already on the verge of losing control of the situation by late April 2011. Advised by a number of IRGC officers present in Syria – including the C-in-C IRGC, Maj Gen Muhammad Ali Jafari, the CO of the IRGC's Quds Force (Jerusalem Corps or Failaq al-Qods in Farsi,

a 'special' formation responsible for 'exporting' Iran's Islamic revolution through 'extraterritorial operations') Maj Gen Qasem Soleimani, and Deputy Director of IRGC Intelligence, Brig Gen Hossein Taeb – it mobilised additional military and intelligence units.[11] These were deployed on the streets, or to surround entire districts and then launch house-to-house raids. Initial targets of such operations were black-listed people, but eventually every male between 14 and 60 became a target.

Unavailingly, related news continued spreading through the entire military and intelligence apparatus, resulting in ever more defections. While no Army units were operating independently, and thus the involved officers, NCOs and soldiers were never able to freely communicate with each other – at least not without attracting attention from omnipresent intelligence operators and loyalists – there was no holding back. First to feel the impact of defections were the 12 special forces regiments: although all deployed at full strength, by early May 2011 all were down to two-thirds strength, some less. For example, the 45th SF Regiment deployed to Banias lost 50 officers and NCOs to defections during April. This regiment was expected to receive support from the 76th Brigade from the 1st AD, but this arrived late because nearly all of its Sunni troops deserted during their march to the coast. The situation in Banias eventually became so critical that the government felt forced to rush the already depleted 53rd SF Regiment, with the help of SyAAF helicopters. The assault on Banias thus began only on 6 May, but then with unprecedented force: the town was encircled by MBTs and APCs while infantry went house-to-house, arresting, summarily executing, looting and raping. When this proved insufficient, the military launched an operation of large-scale ethnic cleansing of all the Sunnis along the coast, forcing tens of thousands of civilians to flee over the mountains into the Idlib Province by the end of May.

The RGD went into action on 4 May, deploying the 555th SF Regiment, parts of the 104th, 105th and 106th Brigades, supported by MBTs and IFVs, to storm the Saqba district in Damascus. Another RGD force raided Douma, killing dozens and arresting hundreds. This division subsequently lost dozens of its officers (including at least one with rank of Lieutenant Colonel) and other ranks to defections, while the CO of the 104th Brigade – Brig Gen Manaf Tlas (son of the former Minister of Defence) – was arrested and later forced to leave the country.

The 1st Armoured Division proved unable to mobilise more than about half of the 76th Brigade, while the cadre of its remaining elements had to hold thousands of Sunni NCOs and soldiers locked in their barracks. The 3rd AD managed to deploy up to two-thirds of all three of its brigades, sending the 65th to Dera'a, the 81st to Zabadani and the 47th to Hama, but by June these units were so depleted by defections that their remnants had to be withdrawn and reorganised as a single brigade deployed in the Dmeyr area. The 5th Mechanised Division was also severely hit by defections and thus able to mobilise only an equivalent of four depleted battalions. The cadre of the 12th Armoured Brigade and the 171st Battalion of the 112th Mechanised Brigade became operational only during June, when they were sent to join what was left of the 59th Battalion of the 132nd Brigade deployed in al-Herak. The 287th Battalion of the 132nd Mechanised Brigade practically melted away in Dera'a, while the 175th Artillery Regiment was never able to leave its base.

A still from a video showing a platoon of BMP-2s from the RGD on the streets of Damascus, in late spring 2011. Rarely seen in public before early 2011, they have become a common sight ever since. (via Tom Cooper)

This still from a video taken by a government soldier shows a concentration of vehicles from the 11th AD somewhere along the highway from Homs to Hama, similar to many such sights in that area during the summer of 2011. In the foreground is a VPV (armoured engineering vehicle with a 6.5t crane), with eight BMP-1s and two T-62Ms in the background. (via R. S.)

The Banias area was to see several waves of massacres and campaigns of ethnic cleansing of Sunnis, all committed by government forces or pro-government Alawite militias, in the 2011–2013 period. This tragic scene was photographed on the outskirts of the town on 4 May 2013. (ENN)

The 7th Armoured Division experienced a spate of defections while attempting to mobilise from its bases along the Golan Heights, and proved capable of deploying only company-sized detachments from the 68th, 78th and 121st Brigades to Zabadani. Even then, the 78th and 121st practically disintegrated: their remnants were reorganised as a task force with about 30 armoured vehicles, later that year, and then re-deployed to Aleppo. The 68th was last reported as still operational in Zabadani, in late 2012, before it was reorganised as a part of the emerging NDF.

START OF THE INSURGENCY

The next major crisis developed in Homs and the nearby town of ar-Rastan – hometown of the Tlas clan – 45km further north. A series of mass protests in Homs during early May prompted the government to deploy a task force consisting of cadres from the 18th, 62nd and 85th Brigades from the 10th Armoured Division into the city (the rest of the 10th AD, that is its 56th Armoured Brigade, was meanwhile rushed to Zabadani). These were reinforced by detachments from the 11th AD. All the elements of these two units were put under the command of companies detached from the 4th AD and under strict control of intelligence services, which established detention camps on at least two football stadiums. After further protests, nearly two-thirds of Homs was put under siege by the military on 5 May.

On 12 May, around 50 soldiers from the 11th Division – many belonging to the Bu Saraya tribe – mutinied and refused to open fire at protesters in front of them. Thirty-five were summarily executed and many others taken away by intelligence operators, never to appear again. State-controlled media subsequently explained that 'Islamist snipers' had attacked 'security forces', and aired purported confessions of 'suspected insurgents' who were forced to say that they had been ordered 'by foreign elements' to attack Syrian soldiers and bomb installations. With Assyrian Christians joining protests, demonstrations continued unabated as government forces opened fire on a funeral procession on 21 May, killing 22.

Meanwhile, the 60th Armoured Brigade from the 11th AD was rushed to ar-Rastan, which developed into another major hot-spot of protest after the local population toppled a statue of Hafez al-Assad and pledged to join the revolution despite a series of brutal raids and hundreds being arrested and killed. During the following days several units of the 18th AD arrived in the area, including the 120th Mechanised Brigade, and the 324th and 990th Battalions – the only elements of the 167th and 134th Armoured Brigades the government managed to mobilise, respectively. All these units were put under the command of a task force from the 4th AD, reinforced by the 45th SF Regiment, and then launched an onslaught on Rastan and nearby town of Talbiseh, in the course of which dozens were killed and hundreds arrested. It was in Rastan and Talbiseh, on 30 May, that small groups of defectors and the local population put up armed resistance to government forces for the first time: unable to enter either, the government reacted by putting both towns under siege and opening artillery fire. More than 200 civilians were killed in this area over the following week, primarily by artillery shelling, but including at least 10 killed when Mi-8 and Mi-25 helicopters rocketed and bombed Rastan for the first time, on 4 June.

By 2 June, protests in Hama had escalated to the point where

Among some of the first Syrian Army defectors who appeared in public was 1st Lieutenant Mohammad Abdul Aziz, who defected with two NCOs from one of the SF regiments in late August 2011. Thousands of Syrian soldiers were to follow in similar fashion, most of them eventually joining the insurgency. (FSA release)

Even the Republican Guards Division has experienced a spate of defections, as disaffected officers and other ranks understood what is actually going on and refused to open fire at civilians protesting and at their comrades in arms. 1st Lieutenant Basil Ali used to serve with the RGD before joining the insurgency in summer 2011. (FSA release)

civilians brought the city centre under their control. This prompted the government to concentrate a number of Army units in the suburbs. These included most of the 47th Armoured Brigade (3rd AD), 68th Armoured Brigade (7th AD), 87th Mechanised Brigade (11th AD), and the 46th and 47th SF Regiments, corseted by task forces from the 42nd Armoured Brigade (4th AD), large groups of Shabiha and several detachments from intelligence services. While advancing on the city centre, the military killed at least 72 protesters on 3 June, and almost as many during funeral processions on the following day.

MUTINY IN JISR ASH-SHUGUR

By early June 2011, morale within the Syrian military in general was on the verge of collapse. No matter how numerous, defections remained limited in size until that time, but the inevitable had to happen sooner or later. Seemingly every city, town and village was meanwhile raided by a platoon or company of MBTs and APCs, usually supported by truck-borne infantry, and there were countless victims of the government's terror. When this did not work, the military began driving their heavy vehicles into the people, like in Dayr az-Zawr on 20 May, where at least a dozen protesters were killed. Amid a rush of reports about such atrocities, the government suddenly launched a claim that 'at least 20 security servicemen' were killed in an ambush and gun battle 'with armed men' in Jisr ash-Shugur, in the Idlib Province, and 'another 37 in an attack on a security post' nearby, on 5 June.

Protesting in Idlib – and in nearby Aleppo Province – did not catch the government by surprise. It had begun already in April, but the first few large scale demonstrations were overpowered by the presence of huge numbers of police officers and intelligence operatives. As the protesting intensified and spread, it was the government that found itself overwhelmed by the task of maintaining the crackdown while trying to prevent local SyAA units from melting away. When the police in Jisr ash-Shugur refused to open fire at protesters, loyalists began executing the policemen – prompting the locally-based Army battalion into mutiny. Intelligence operatives managed to summarily execute more than 50 mutineers before they were overpowered by the

rest of the SyAA battalion. The mutineers armed themselves with weapons captured from police stations and military bases and were then joined by defectors from other military bases in the area. Eventually, this first group of genuine – and entirely native – Syrian insurgents grew to more than 2,000 defectors, led by SyAA officers who declared themselves 'free'.

A quick reaction and brutal – and complete – crushing of such mutinies was of utmost importance for the government, which insisted on maintaining the image of a military that was free of fracturing. Therefore, elements of the 4th AD under the command of Brig Gen Sharif were rushed from Dera'a towards Jisr ash-Shugur, followed by one SF regiment and what was left of the 76th Brigade. The 4th AD was temporarily stopped on the Orontes River because insurgents blew up several bridges. Reinforced by the 35th SF Regiment, the loyalists eventually managed to approach the town and then launched an unprecedented campaign of terror: they not only sought out and summarily executed any deserter they could find, but slaughtered entire families, then streets and neighbourhoods, looting and burning not only houses and stores but also crop fields. Resistance was fierce and losses heavy, prompting the government to deploy the 46th and 555th SF Regiments into the area, followed by the 85th Brigade, in order to enable an assault from two directions.[12] Starting on 10 June, SyAAF helicopters flew some 30 combat sorties against insurgents in Jisr ash-Shugur, and later that day most of the town was in government hands again. Much of the population – an estimated 50,000 people – fled towards the Turkish border, with regime forces in hot pursuit: the majority of the defectors and hundreds of civilians were never seen again.

The situation in Ma'arat an-Numaan developed in similar fashion: the Army unit there refused to open fire on protesters and the regime reacted by deploying the 556th SF Regiment with the help of Mi-8 helicopters, which subsequently attacked protesters and mutineers with unguided rockets. In the course of ensuing street battles the insurgents claimed the first SyAAF Mi-8 helicopter as shot down, on 10 June.

Similar scenes were taking place in Homs and Hama: parts of the 68th Brigade (7th ID) mutinied and the unit was withdrawn

A SyAAF Mi-8MT (serial number 1299) flies low over the northern Hama Province in mid-2011, when the type was heavily utilised for transportation of special forces, but also for some of the first aerial attacks on protesters and mutineers. Notable are hardpoints on the side of the cabin, often used for bombs up to a calibre of 250kg and UV-16-57 rocket pods. (Photo by YoungHamwiLens, via R. S.)

from the city. The majority of officers and other ranks who deserted fled in the direction of the Idlib Province. Parts of the 67th Armoured Brigade in Homs then defected too – taking with them at least one operational T-55 MBT plus a cache of machine guns and RGP-7s (anti-tank rocket-propelled grenades) – to join insurgent groups in Rastan and Talbiseh. In both cases, the government reacted by launching an outright manhunt with the help of Mi-8/17 helicopters and special forces. However, this operation was not as successful as the one in Idlib: still under the impression of news related to the death of Hamza al-Khatib, on 10 June defectors in Rastan announced the establishment of the 1st Free Brigade and their intention to resist attacks by the government. A day later, they claimed two SyAAF helicopters as shot down around Talbiseh.

4
SPREAD OF THE INSURGENCY

Massacres of protesters and atrocities against the civilian population by government forces finally began prompting some diplomatic pressure against the government in Damascus during mid-June 2011.[13] However, insisting on his version of a 'foreign conspiracy', President Assad only reacted with orders for additional – and ever more brutal - crackdowns. Obviously, the spate of defections from the SyAA during May and June did have an impact in that the government was forced to realise it was lacking enough loyal and reliable military forces to establish a permanent presence in all of the country. Indeed, it was lacking the detention facilities necessary to keep tens of thousands of detainees arrested in the meantime, and forces necessary to keep most of the Army locked within its barracks. Correspondingly, most of the subsequent raids were of rather short duration: loyalist forces would drive through a village, town or neighbourhood, arrest whoever they could catch, summarily execute a few black-listed people and then loot homes and shops. However, none of involved units could stay in the same place for longer than two or three days before they would receive orders for raiding another locality. Therefore, not

only such hot-spots as Dera'a or Rastan, but also large parts of Damascus, Homs, Hama, Aleppo and Lattakia saw no government presence for days, in turn enabling the opposition to recover, then improve its organisation and spread its influence. During late June and through July, this resulted not only in a wave of the biggest demonstrations in the history of the country, but also a paralysed economy. After the governor of Hama was forced out of the city, well over 200,000 participated in the 'Friday of Lost Legitimacy' protest on 24 June, when the first large-scale protests took place in central Damascus too. Southern and eastern Aleppo experienced a series of protests a week later, when up to 100,000 participated in about two dozen demonstrations organised in different districts of the city. During July, several huge demonstrations – some including between 600,000 and 750,000 people – took place in Hama and Lattakia, while an entire wave of mass demonstrations swept through all of southern and eastern Damascus. Similarly, between 200,000 and 350,000 people were regularly protesting in Dayr az-Zawr.

While continuing the crackdown, the government solved a part of its problems by releasing thousands of political prisoners. Although most such decisions were presented in the media as attempts at reconciliation, what was little known at that time is that very few of the released detainees were activists and those in opposition involved in protesting in 2011: the majority were members of the Moslem Brotherhood and various other Islamists held for many years.

RAMADAN MASSACRE

With the nearing of the holy month of Ramadan, the opposition further intensified protesting during August, hoping this might reach the level where the government would finally give up. Before long it became perfectly clear that such hopes were naive. On the evening of 24 July, a mutiny erupted at the Military College in Homs. Precise details about this remain largely unknown because not one of the several hundred instructors and cadets involved survived. However, the situation was serious enough for the government to concentrate two SF regiments supported by elements of two armoured brigades and helicopter

Many of the military's attacks on protests were launched under the disguise of 'police operations against terrorists'. Because of this, dozens of SyAA BRDM-2 armoured scout cars – including this example photographed in November 2011 - received quasi-police camouflage patterns and corresponding inscriptions. (via R. S.)

A SyAA BMP-1 under way outside Homs. As usual, the camouflage pattern – consisting of original green colour in which the vehicle was delivered, with large splotches of orange sand applied in Syria – is badly worn out. Unit insignia and vehicle serials are usually applied on the glacis plate and rear entry doors. (via R. S.)

This still from a video shows a typical Army checkpoint in Homs, some time during the second half of 2011, including two T-55s and a ZSU-23-4 Shilka, positioned to control the surrounding area in two directions. (via M.Z.)

Major Manhal Aslaadaa defected with a number of other soldiers from the 137th Mechanised Brigade, together with one of the BMP-1s under his command, to the insurgent side in Dayr az-Zawr in August 2011. (FSA release)

gunships to assault the compound. Whoever survived this attack was summarily executed.

Simultaneously, a major crisis erupted in Dayr az-Zawr, where the newly-appointed governor was forced out of the city by protesters, while parts of the 137th Armoured Brigade (17th AD) mutinied and clashed with militias of the AFI and SMA. The government reacted on 30 July, deploying all available mechanised forces in Homs and Hama to launch offensives on

these cities, both of which were put under siege, with electricity, food and water supplies cut off. Still small in size and only lightly armed, local insurgent groups were largely overwhelmed by this onslaught. In sporadic ambushes they claimed the destruction of about a dozen armoured vehicles and several passenger buses carrying government troops. For example, the Commando Battalion of the Khalid Ibn al-Wallid Brigade of the Free Syrian Army (FSA) ambushed a convoy of about 30 vehicles inside Homs, late on 30 July, killing and injuring nearly 50 troops. In Hama, the FSA ambushed several advancing convoys, destroying a number of armoured vehicles and assassinating Brig Gen Dargham, the director of SMA in that city. Rallying his remaining troops, the CO of the 11th AD, Maj Gen Zaitoun, eventually managed to overpower the resistance by 7 August, although not without support from heliborne-deployed commandos and at least 12 Mi-8s deployed as gunships. Eventually, the insurgents were forced to withdraw. Once free to operate, the military and intelligence operatives conducted two weeks of house-to-house raids, arresting thousands and summarily executing up to 1,200 people, which is why this period became known as the 'Ramadan Massacre'.

Similar operation was undertaken in Dayr az-Zawr, where demonstrations turned into rioting that left most police stations looted and burned out on 31 July. President Assad removed Minister of Defence Ali Habib – who was personally in charge of operations in that city – and replaced him with Lt Gen Abdullah Dawoud Rajiha, and then ordered the military into action. On 6 August the 137th Mechanised Brigade (17th AD) – corseted by a full brigade of PSD – deployed three columns to launch an advance into Dayr az-Zawr. While one of columns was ambushed by insurgents and forced to retreat in disarray, another quickly changed sides and joined protesters – together with all of its heavy armament. Only the third column – consisting of the cadre of the 119th Mechanised Battalion – managed to reach the town centre and the Military Hospitals. Once there, this unit was encircled by insurgents and fiercely attacked, suffering more than 200 casualties. The government's hold on Dayr az-Zawr never recovered from this blow. Although survivors of the 119th Battalion were saved by heliborne deployed special forces, supported by air strikes flown by SyAAF MiG-21s on the morning of 10 August, and this force remained in control of the town centre and the air base outside the city, the eastern side of Dayr az-Zawr has ever since been under insurgent control.

FREE SYRIAN ARMY

Hopes that the holy month of Ramadan might prove a turning point and the regime could be overthrown peacefully were practically smashed by the terror of government forces. Some Syrian activists subsequently adapted their tactics and resorted to 'flash protests': short-duration, small scale demonstrations organised primarily by night, which swiftly dispersed before being continued – shortly after – by new gatherings in another place. Large-scale protesting was continued only in places with a lesser military presence, like Idlib, Raqqa and especially Dayr az-Zawr. Other activists began joining thousands of military deserters and – concluding that the government and its die-hard supporters remained unimpressed by protests and mass defections, and were unlikely to give up – began calling for an organised armed response. One of the results was the establishment of the Free Syrian Army, announced to the public on 29 July 2011.

The original officer cadre of the FSA envisaged it as an apolitical, non-sectarian and non-religious insurgent force for the protection of civilian protest, without political goals other than the removal of Assad's government. Hundreds of its early operations were aimed at government forces threatening protesters or involved in attacks on them, or in the process of deploying to places of protest.

The FSA experienced a period of significant expansion during the second half of 2011, when a steady flow of Army defectors enabled the establishment of dozens of new units. By September 2011, armed groups that declared themselves the FSA were operating in all Syrian provinces, but foremost in Aleppo and Idlib, Homs, Hama and Rastan in the centre of the country, Dera'a and Houran in the south, and Dayr az-Zawr and al-Bukamal in the east. Homs and Rastan were major areas of recruitment and defections there reached proportions where the FSA established its first two 'brigades' – named the Khalid Ibn al-Wallid and Sallahaddin Victorye. However, many defectors preferred to join their families instead of the insurgency and most brought only light infantry weapons – primarily AK-47s, DShK machine guns and RPG-7s – with them. Smaller numbers of various assault rifles of Western origin were acquired via Lebanon and Libya (some even from purchased from Shabiha smugglers). Therefore, for most of 2011 the insurgency lacked heavier weapons.

During mid-September 2011, the government was busy sweeping Jabal az-Zawiya area of Idlib – where dozens of defectors were killed and many Sunni villages depopulated – Damascus and Rif Dimashq (where even Christians came under attack when they dared to protest). Towards the end of that month, different task forces converged on Rastan, which came under renewed attack on 28 September. The local FSA battalions destroyed a handful of vehicles and caused up to 50 casualties before being forced to withdraw in the direction of Homs. By mid-October, the insurgents established themselves in *de-facto* control of several districts of the latter city, where they were joined by additional defectors (including around 100 officers and soldiers of the 60th and 67th Brigades). Understanding that it was facing a popular uprising, the government scrambled detachments from the 4th AD, intelligence agencies and Shabiha to save what was left of the 10th AD. However, its next major operation, launched on 23 October, encountered fierce resistance from the Khalid Ibn al-Wallid Brigade. These not only destroyed a number of BMP-1 IFVs and BTR-60 APCs and caused over 250 casualties, but also prompted another wave of defections and eventually brought the Bab Amr and Khalidya districts under their control.

The near-simultaneous crisis in Homs, intensive fighting in Rastan, Qusayr, Dayr az-Zawr and al-Boukamal (in eastern Syria) that lasted for days, continuous defections from Army units, the emergence of the FSA and also numerous local self-defence militias all over the country apparently overwhelmed the government. Instead of launching the usual raids and sweeps, the loyalists put Bab Amr and Khalidya districts under siege: they were occasionally shelled by artillery and – on 30 October – even experienced the first air strike flown by a pair of Su-22s, but otherwise loyalists troops limited their activity to driving MBTs and IFVs up and down the main streets, shooting randomly. It was only in mid-November– after the entire 138th Brigade from the 4th AD was deployed from Tartous to Homs and Rastan – that large scale assaults were launched. Parts of the Khalid Ibn al-Wallid Brigade were encircled and suffered heavy losses, including at least 16 KIA – between them some of the officers who founded the FSA – and 50 wounded, but Bab Amr and Khalidya remained under insurgent control.

These soldiers defected to the FSA together with their BMP-1 amid heavy fighting in the Khalidya district of Homs in late 2011. (SNN)

BATTLES OF ZABADANI AND HOMS

Following weeks of anti-government protesting, on 7 January 2012 elements of the 56th Brigade (10th AD), corseted by parts of the 4th AD and intelligence operatives, were deployed to assault Zabadani, a town some 30km north of Damascus and very close to the border with Lebanon, surrounded by high mountains – and the HQ of the II Corps SyAA. This operation back-fired, because parts of the 56th Brigade defected and turned their weapons against loyalists. The government regrouped and launched a new counterattack on 13 January, but this was beaten back with a loss of four T-55s, at least one BMP-1 and about 50 casualties. After both sides agreed to a ceasefire on 18 January, Zabadani became the first Syrian town under insurgent control.

Although agreeing to withdraw the military, Bashar al-Assad was not prepared to accept the loss of Zabadani. During the second half of January a new task force was created from a battalion of the 4th AD reinforced by company-sized detachments from different units of the 81st Brigade (3rd AD), 62nd Brigade (10th Division), and 7th Division, before launching a new attack on 4 February. This time, the loyalist commanders were extremely careful: detachments from regular Army units were not left to approach Zabadani, but tasked with providing artillery support, outer cordon and clearing the restive valley around the town. After two days of bombardment, the 4th AD, reinforced by at least one SF regiment, launched its assault. The fighting was bitter and it took the loyalists five days to overcome insurgent resistance in Madaya and reach Zabadani, on 11 February, before continuing with house-to-house raids that lasted several days. Although the majority of insurgents managed to escape into the nearby hills, hundreds were arrested and many summarily executed.

While still fighting for Zabadani, the government attempted to crush the uprising in Homs. What was left of locally-deployed elements of the 11th and 18th Divisions was reinforced by a battalion each from the 104th and 105th Brigades RGB, the 42nd and 138th Brigades of the 4th AD, the 53rd and 556th SF Regiments of the 14th Division, and the 45th, 54th and 555th SF Regiments of the 15th Division. Under the command of Maj Gen al-Ali of the RGD, this nearly corps-sized force first encircled the city before cutting off all water supplies, electricity and communications on 3 February. While other units dug a two-metre deep trench around districts held by insurgents, and shelled Bab Amr and Khalidya, the 4th AD established a large number of checkpoints at which any male civilian aged between 14 and 60 was arrested. The Farouq Brigade FSA reacted with a series of attacks on checkpoints and bases, causing dozens of casualties, and managing to hold the loyalists at bay for days, but in return the shelling caused hundreds of civilian and insurgent casualties, including one of its leading commanders, Col Ahmed Jumrek, killed on 10 February.

On 13 February, the 555th SF regiment, supported by the 404th Armoured Regiment (both from the 15th Division), launched the first assault on Bab Amr. Lacking training and experience in operations in a complicated urban setting, the loyalists were easily beaten back with the loss of at least four BMP-1s and a number of killed. While licking its wounds, and adding the 35th and 127th SF regiments, and the 85th Brigade (10th Division) to its concentration of forces in Homs, the government continued

A gathering of Army defectors-cum-insurgents in the Zabadani area in January 2012. (FSA release)

A BMP-1 knocked out during the second attack on Zabadani on 13 January 2013. (FSA release)

This T-55 from the 7th AD was photographed on the outskirts of Zabadani in February 2013. (via R. S.)

shelling Bab Amr for several days before the next attempt. On 23 February its units pushed into the Jobar area near Bab Amr, though not without suffering significant losses in the process. However, hardest hit was the local population and a large number of refugees, hundreds of whom were either killed by shelling or kidnapped and summarily executed by the loyalists.

The main attack on Bab Amr was launched by special forces

This 'police'-marked BRDM-2 of the SyAA was knocked out together with at least one BMP-1 during an insurgent attack on a government checkpoint at Cairo Square in Homs in February 2012. (SNN)

A T-72AV of the 4th AD knocked out by insurgents while attempting to advance into the Khaldiya district of Homs in early 2012. (via M.Z.)

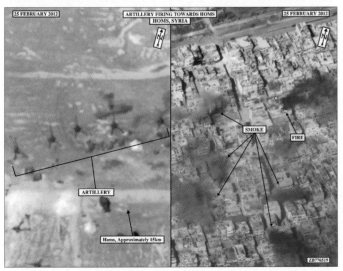

Satellite intelligence photographs released by the US Department of Defence showing artillery positions and traces of intensive shelling of Homs by loyalist forces in February 2012. (US DoD)

supported by around 30 MBTs and IFVs on 29 February, after additional shelling and several attacks by helicopter gunships. With at least 114 out of about 250 insurgents of the Farouq Brigade FSA killed, Bab Amr was overrun by government forces on the morning of 1 March. Next, a government task force of similar size and composition attacked Karm al-Zeitoun, on 9 March, and Bab Sbaa, on 24 March. Once again, the loyalists suffered significant losses in the course of these operations, including at least six MBTs and IFVs, and one Mi-8 claimed as shot down on 10 March over Karm al-Zeitoun. However, with this the insurgents had run themselves out of steam: already weakened by months of siege and heavy fighting, they were forced to withdraw, and by the time a nationwide ceasefire was announced on 1 April, the government was in control of 13 out of 16 Sunni districts of Homs.

Apparently, by deploying a huge concentration of forces inside the city, the government cleared the strongest point of insurgent resistance up to that time, secured the crucial crossroad of highways between Damascus, Aleppo and the coast, and prevented the insurgency in Homs from regaining momentum for the rest of that year. However, according to SANA releases for the period between January and March 2012, it can be reliably concluded that the government suffered a loss of nearly 1,000 KIA in Homs.[14] Furthermore, resistance never ceased completely, and the SyAA engineers were finally forced to construct a three-metre high cement barrier around Bab Amr, leaving only a few narrow gaps for entry or exit, all protected by heavily fortified checkpoints. So while securing much of the city, the offensive actually tied down much of what was left of the SyAA at the time: the government was badly short of military units. Indeed, a large proportion of what is left of the Army remains concentrated in the Homs area and tied to the task of securing strategic highways from Damascus to the coast to this day.

LAST SYAA OFFENSIVES

Outside Homs the FSA remained unsuccessful, illustrating the inability of the government to maintain a sufficient troop presence just 40km away from that city. During November and December 2011, a series of protests culminated in the near-liberation of al-Qusayr, a town of around 70,000 near the border with Lebanon. After destroying most checkpoints on the outskirts, the insurgents attacked into the town centre on 13 February 2012, and destroyed the local HQ of the AFI, forcing a garrison of about 400 intelligence operatives and Shabiha to withdraw. The government rushed a company of T-62s from the 85th Brigade to Qusayr, but at least one of the crews involved defected and knocked out three other tanks in a short battle, in turn enabling the FSA to secure the entire town. The loyalists subsequently deployed reinforcements around Qusayr but – lacking the troop strength for an assault – only put it under a siege, starting on 4 March 2012.

During the spring of 2012, the insurgency spread through the southern outskirts of Damascus and the surrounding Rif Dimashq Province. The government deployed the Republican Guards Division and much of the 4th AD, supported by operatives of all major intelligence agencies, to run a series of savage raids through Douma, Erbeen, Rankoos, Zamalka, Jisreen and Harasta. Although suffering extensive losses in armour, the military re-established itself in control of most of these, and local insurgents admitted to have withdrawn by the end of March.

Assad next ordered the military to recover the city of Idlib, a stronghold of protest through early 2012 and practically under insurgent control, and re-open road links between Lattakia and Aleppo. Furthermore, there was a necessity to secure the Abu ad-Duhor AB, south-east of Idlib, where mutiny erupted on 3 March, when a group of about 50 officers and other ranks attempted to defect. The 35th, 46th and 47th SF Regiments and the 76th Armoured Brigade – a total of about 3,000 troops supported by some 40 armoured vehicles, corseted by elements of the 4th AD (including most of the 145th Artillery Regiment) and intelligence services – were deployed in this direction the same month. After bringing the situation at Abu ad-Duhor AB under control on 10 March, the military began shelling Idlib with artillery and mortars, and then launched an infantry assault supported by T-72s and BMP-1s. The insurgents easily ambushed several mechanised columns as these drove towards the centre of the town, claiming at least six destroyed tanks and one helicopter as shot down, but casualties were heavy on both sides, with more than 100 combatants and civilians killed before the surviving insurgents withdrew towards Binnish on 13 March.

During the rest of that month and April, the 76th AB was deployed in additional 'search and destroy' operations along the road from Idlib to Aleppo, committing numerous atrocities and even leaving behind graffiti proclaiming these as work of the 'Death Brigade' – a nickname that sticks to this unit to this day. However, it suffered such losses in the process that it repeatedly had to be bolstered through transfer of predominantly Alawite-staffed companies from other units that fell apart. Following in its wake, the remnants of the 46th SF Regiment then established 'Base 46', overlooking large stretches of that road, in an attempt to secure this vital supply link.

While mass protesting in Aleppo, Damascus, Hama and Dayr az-Zawr continued, the tempo of the government's military operations apparently slowed down during May, June and July. Actually, dozens of small task forces remained active all over the country, often in response to demonstrations, but more often in outright massacres of the Sunni population in Homs, Hama and Idlib Provinces, instigated in order to scare others into fleeing. More importantly, when loyalist troops returned to re-raid some towns they faced stiff resistance from insurgents. Many columns moving towards Idlib were ambushed while passing through Ariha, with heavy loss. What was subsequently left of the Syrian military in Idlib Province was reduced to holding that city, a thin corridor along the road to Lattakia and a number of isolated bases and checkpoints distributed along a few other roads in the area.

A T-62M (probably from the 11th AD), captured by insurgents (or brought by one of the defectors) outside al-Qusayr in February 2012. (SNN via Y.A.)

T-55 tanks from one of the units subordinated to the notorious 76th – or 'Death' – Brigade advancing along Route 58, in the Idlib Province, in 2012. Rugged terrain provided plenty of opportunity for ambushes, and these were repeatedly exploited by insurgents. (ENN)

From these relatively secure bases, loyalists were able to shell opposition-controlled areas from a distance, applying methods of collective punishment of the population that supported insurgency. However, they ceased launching patrols in order not to expose themselves to ambushes. This and the decision to maintain these thinly-stretched units was obviously driven by the need to maintain a presence in order to maintain the government's claim to power. In turn, this made it necessary to conserve what was left of the military's combat power, because the insurgents were thus forced to engage well dug-in troops, protected by strong defences, armoured vehicles and artillery, and supported from the air. The strongpoints had the additional benefit of isolating less reliable troops from contact with the population and reducing the likelihood of defection. However, this also meant that the government did nothing to disrupt insurgent activity in the countryside, enabling them to expand their forces to brigade-level organisations and establish good supply links to Turkey.

Developments in the al-Qusayr area followed a similar pattern. On 31 May, a task force consisting of elements from the 65th AB (3rd AD) and 4th AD launched an attack on the town, only to run into numerous ambushes set up by insurgents led by defected officers from special forces regiments. By the time they were forced to stop their assault, on 9 June, the loyalists left behind at least eight knocked out T-72s and over 200 casualties. Overall, government forces suffered a loss of at least 33 BMP-1s destroyed and 13 captured by insurgents, and 20 different MBTs destroyed

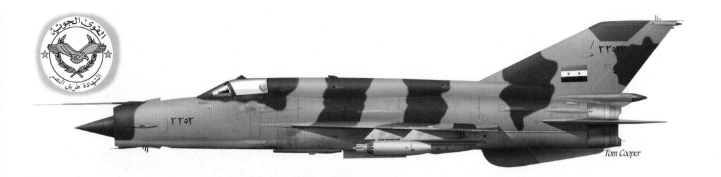

Rarely seen in action early on during the war, the fleet of about 60 MiG-21bis flew more than 1,000 registered combat sorties between 1 October 2012 and 30 April 2013. All the aircraft still in service underwent overhauls at 'The Works', where they were painted in different variants of the camouflage pattern illustrated here. This consists of dark yellow sand and blue-green on the top surfaces and sides, and light admiralty grey or light blue on the bottom surfaces. National markings are worn on six positions (including fin flashes). All are equipped with chaff and flare dispensers, apparently of indigenous design, attached to the lower fuselage. (Tom Cooper)

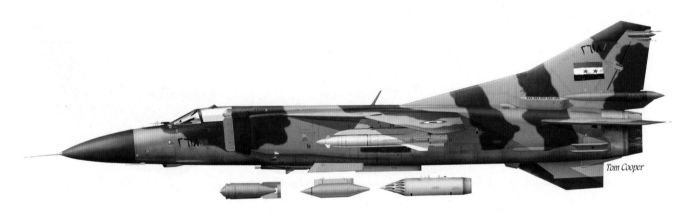

A reconstruction of a MiG-23MF (serial number 2618) as sighted (and photographed) over the Aleppo and Idlib Provinces on several occasions during late 2013. Painted in the same colours like all of the SyAAF MiG-21s, and applied in pattern that's different from aircraft to aircraft, it is illustrated with the fin flash, as applied very often on Syrian combat aircraft, in a rather crude fashion. The plane is shown armed with a Kh-23M guided missile, such as during attack on the HQ of Tawhid Brigade in northern Aleppo, in late 2013, which killed much of that unit's staff. Insets are showing two other major types of weapons deployed by this variant, including a FAB-250M54 general-purpose bomb, Delta pod (for guiding Kh-23 missile), and a B-8M rocket pod. (Tom Cooper)

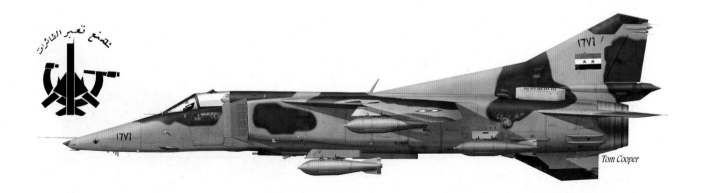

A reconstruction of the MiG-23BN (serial number 1679), as seen over Damascus in early 2013, while carrying six FAB-500M-62 general-purpose bombs. Like all locally overhauled MiG-23MFs, Syrian MiG-23BNs are equipped with large boxes containing chaff and flare dispensers, installed on the top of the rear fuselage, on either side of the fin. Inset is the insignia of 'The Works' at Nayrab AB, applied on nearly all aircraft and helicopters that are overhauled there. (Tom Cooper)

One of the SyAAF MiG-29s overhauled by 'The Works' at Nayrab IAP is this example, serialled 3432. Although relatively fresh, its camouflage pattern appears not to be of very good quality because it was rapidly bleached by the sun and sand. Syrian MiG-29s have been upgraded with a new weapons system which makes them compatible with R-77 (AA-11 Adder) medium-range air-to-air missiles and a wide range of PGMs, including the Kh-29T (AS-14 Kedge). (Tom Cooper)

A reconstruction of the SyAAF Su-22M-3K (serial number 2527). Originally camouflaged in brown and dark green, most of these aircraft have been overhauled by 'The Works' at Nayrab AB, where they were re-painted in different camouflage patterns consisting of colours standardised by the SyAAF. All have been modified to carry chaff and flare dispensers of indigenous design on the top of the rear fuselage. The aircraft is illustrated as armed with B-8M pods for unguided rockets, calibre 80mm, as introduced to service on advice of Iranian instructors. At earlier times, the type was usually armed with older and less effective UB-16-57 pods or FAB-250M-62 general-purpose bombs. (Tom Cooper)

The relatively small fleet of 21 Su-24MKs, operated by No. 819 Squadron SyAAF from T.4 air base, is probably the most heavily utilised part of SyAAF's fighter-bomber fleet. Between 1 October 2012 and 30 April 2013, about a dozen of these aircraft that are available on average (a similar number was still undergoing overhauls in Russia) flew no less than 400 registered combat sorties. Camouflaged in Russian colours known as 667 Brown and 670 Light Brown on the top surfaces, the aircraft is most often armed with the FAB-250M-62, as shown here, a maximum of 10 of which can be installed at once (including two on a dual launcher on the inboard underwing pylon). (Tom Cooper)

The fleet of about 150 Mi-8s and Mi-17s was probably the most heavily utilised part of the SyAAF in this conflict. It suffered the heaviest losses too, with more than 60 helicopters being shot down or knocked out on the ground between June 2011 and December 2013. Most SyAAF Mi-8s are painted in these colours, applied in very different patterns on every helicopter that was overhauled by 'The Works' at Nayrab AB, and which are often strongly bleached by the sun and sand. Serial number 1255 was captured by insurgents at Afis AB. It is illustrated with an assortment of weapons usually deployed by this type, including one of the fearful 'Barmil' improvised bombs, UV-16-57 rocket pod and two variants of RBK-250 cluster bombs. Additional insets show the housing for Doppler radar and a chaff and flare dispenser as installed under the boom of some helicopters, and an alternative fin flash. (Tom Cooper)

A reconstruction of the Mi-25 (serial number 2851) shot down west of Dayr az-Zawr on 6 May 2013 (the crew, including pilot Col Ahmed Yahya, gunner Lt Abdel Karim Ibrahim Ibn Nasser and technician Sgt Salman Asif Derg, was killed). Insets show details of various weapons deployed by Syrian Mi-25s, including a 9-A-624 gun pod (with 23mm calibre cannon), FAB-100-120 and FAB-250M54 general-purpose bombs, OFAB-250ShN and ODAB-500 incendiary bombs – all of Russian origin. (Tom Cooper)

In late October 2013, the Army of Islam announced that it had made operational two L-39s captured at Ksheesh AB – probably with the help of veterans from the UAE or Qatari military. The aircraft were test-rolled on the runway but seem never to have been flown or pressed into combat. This is a reconstruction of one of the two L-39s in question, based on videos and photos released by the AI. The aircraft appears to have been completely overpainted in sand and light green on the upper surfaces and sides, and has got the AI's logo applied on the tops of the fins. Serial number 2111 was probably taken over from the SyAAF. (Tom Cooper)

A modified T-72AV of the 105th Brigade RGD in the Harasta area in 2012. Syria signed a contract with Italian company Galileo Avionica (a wholly-owned subsidiary of Finmeccanica) in 1998, envisaging an upgrade of 124 T-72M1s and T-72AVs to this standard, which includes the installation of the Galileo Tank Universal Reconfiguration Modular System (for) T-series tank fire-control system – 'TURMS-T'. This system includes stabilised sights for the gunner and commander, infra-red cameras and a new turret-management computer, improving the gun stabilisation and accuracy. Syrian TURMS-T T-72s are capable of firing the Russian-made 9K119 Reflex (AT-11) ATGMs through their main 125mm calibre guns. (Radek Panchartek)

The primary MBT of armoured and mechanised formations of the RGD and the 4th AD were T-72AVs, some 500 of which were obtained by Syria in the 1990s. Those of the 4th AD were usually painted in olive green. The example shown here was handed over to (Lebanese) Hezbollah, in early 2014. (Radek Panchartek)

This T-72 was captured by insurgents of the Farouq Brigade together with about a dozen others when they overran the base of the 34th Armoured Brigade in Halfaya (Hama Province) in December 2012. Most were subsequently pressed into service, but many were lost due to lack of fuel and spares – and to attacks by SyAAF Mi-25s. The camouflage applied on this T-72 is quite 'typical' for most vehicles of this type in service with the Syrian Army, consisting of the original olive green enhanced through the addition of stripes and splotches of dark yellow sand. (Radek Panchartek)

A T-62M captured by insurgents in Idlib Province in February 2012. The SyAA fleet of T-62s was painted in many different patterns and colours, but the one shown here – consisting of the original olive green, enhanced with large splotches of dark yellow sand – was most widespread in 2013. (Radek Panchartek)

This is one of about a dozen T-55s operated by the Islamic Front's 'Tank Brigade' in Aleppo Province in late 2013. The original olive green camouflage colour was largely worn out, and enhanced by splotches of dark yellow sand and stripes in light sand colours, applied on the sides of the tank and the turret, but not on top surfaces. The inscription on the turret side identifies this vehicle as operated by the Islamic Front. (Radek Panchartek)

This T-55AMV of the 5th MD was sighted in Dera'a in April 2011 and is typical for the look of most vechicles of this variant operated since by mechanised divisions of the Syrian Arab Army. The AMV is an upgraded variant of the earlier T-55AM, including a new engine and new radios, mainly recognisable by the attachment of ERA armour on the turret and hull-sides. (Radek Panchartek)

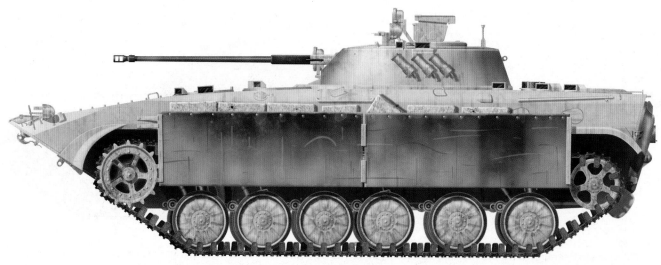

Syria purchased only about 100 BMP-2s, starting in 1987, and these serve with the 104th and 106th Brigades RGD (none have been sighted in company with TURMS-T-modified T-72s of the 105th Brigade so far). Equipped with the stabilised 2A42 automatic 30mm calibre cannon, the BMP-2 proved quite a successful design, handy even in fighting in urban areas. Nevertheless, due to lack of native troops, most BMP-2s that remain operational are now used by IRGC-led units of Iraqi Shi'a and a few even by Hezbollah, and many have received improvised rubber skirts (or mesh/slat armour) for better protection from RPGs. (Radek Panchartek)

The Syrian Arab Army used to operate large numbers of BMP-1s in all of its armoured and mechanised formations, camouflaged in a wide range of different patterns. This example was captured by insurgents of the 'Dawn of Islam Brigade' (as indicated by the inscription on its side) in Ma'arat an-Numaan in October 2012. (Radek Panchartek)

Each brigade of the SyAAF used to operate at least a battery of ZSU-23-4 'Shilka' self-propelled, four-barrelled, radar-controlled anti-aircraft 23mm calibre cannons. Most were camouflaged in this fashion, through the application of splotches of yellow sand over their original olive green colour (notably, some units used stencils for application of the dark yellow sand colour, so that all splotches around the vehicle were in exactly the same shape!). (Radek Panchartek)

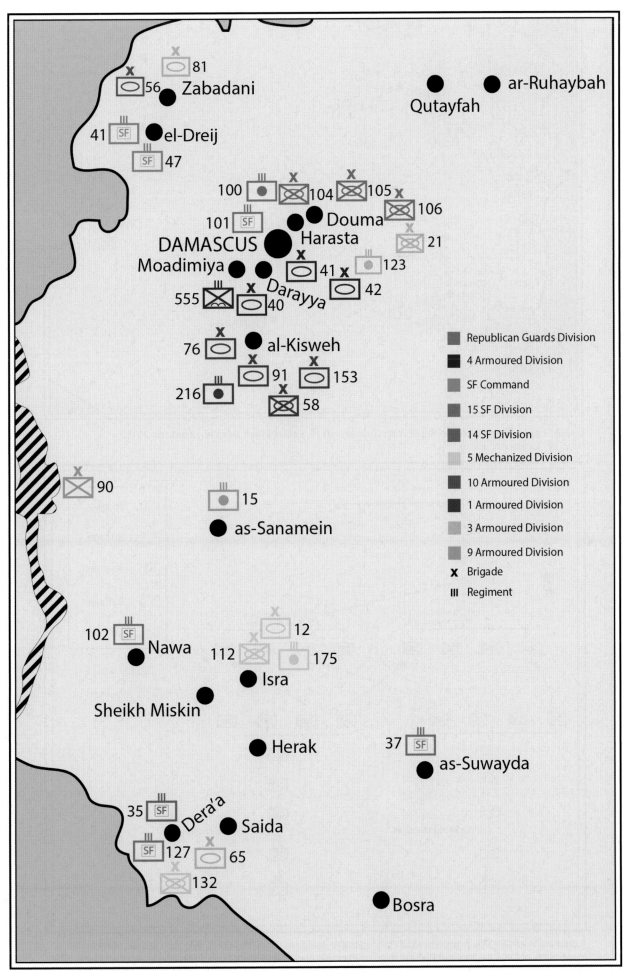

Dispositions of major SyAA and Republican Guards units in south-western Syria as of March-April 2011.
(Map by George Anderson)

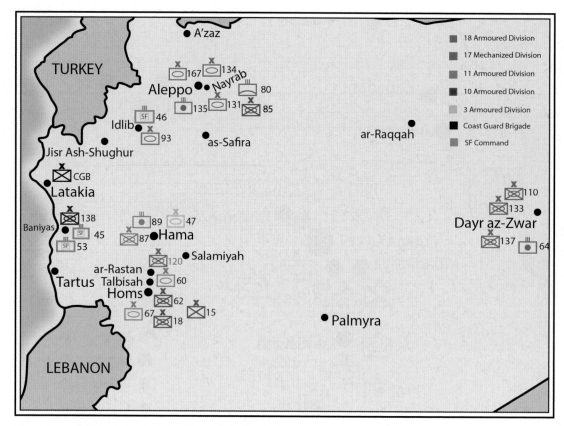

Dispositions of major SyAA and Republican Guards units in north-western Syria as of autumn 2011.
(Map by George Anderson)

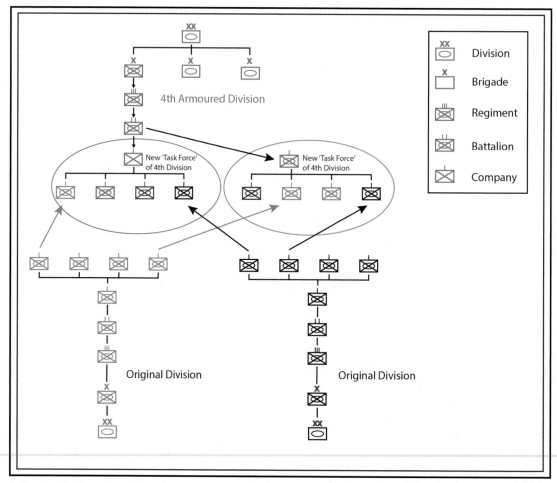

A diagram illustrating the fashion in which the regime re-assigned remaining loyal units from various army divisions to elements of the 4th Armoured Division in order to create about two dozen 'task forces',during April and June 2011. Necessitated by widespread defections and several mutinies within the military, this resulted in the emergence of numerous units usually declared as elements of the 4th Armoured Division - although task forces in question largely consisted of companies, battalions, regiments and brigade-headquarters from other divisions.
(Diagram by George Anderson)

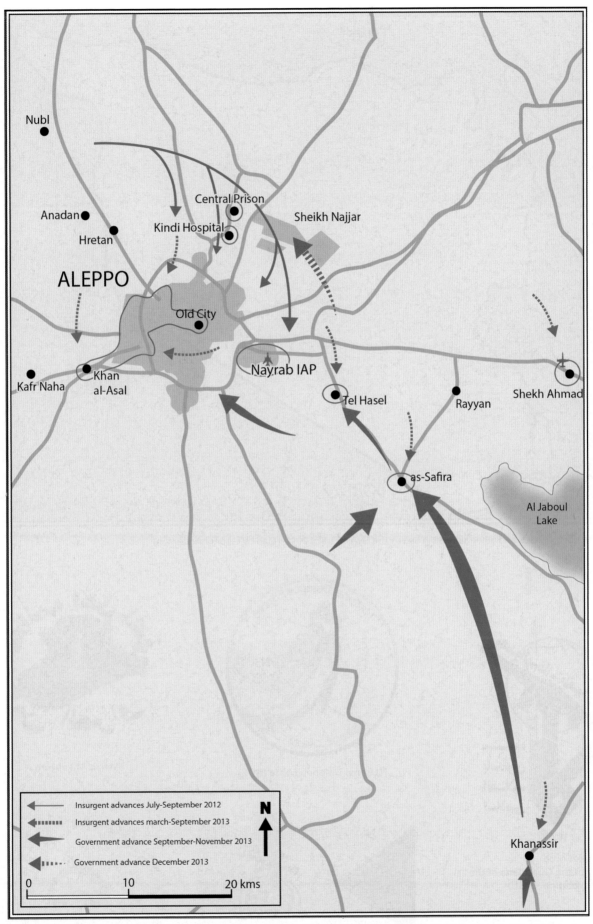

A map of the battle for Aleppo, fought between late July 2012, and into the autumn of 2013. The initial insurgent sweep (marked in green) saw large parts of northern and eastern Aleppo coming under their control. Between March and September 2013, insurgents have cut off the regime-held western Aleppo and encircled the international airport. Only the IRGC-led counteroffensive via Khanassir and as-Safira (red arrows), run between September and November 2013, re-established the land connection with western Aleppo and subsequently enabled the regime to envelop much of the insurgent-held areas in the east of the largest Syrian city. (Map by George Anderson)

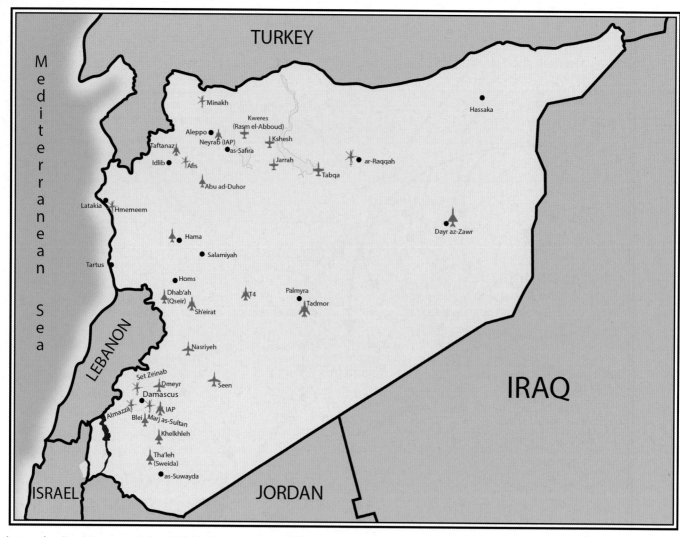

A map of major air bases and other airfields in use by the SyAAF as of 2011. (Map by George Anderson)

Quds Corps/Force
(the Army of the Guardians of the
Islamic Revolution, IRGC)

National Defence Force (NDF)

Asa'ib Ahl al-Haq

Hezbollah Brigades

Kata'ib Sayyid ash-Shuhada

Promised Day Brigades (PDB)

Abu Fadl al-Abbas Brigade (LAFA)

Zulfiqar Brigade

Syrian Social Nationalist Party (SSNP)

Army of Monotheists (or Unitarians)

Palestine Liberation Army (PLA)

Popular Front for the Liberation of Palestine – General Command (PFLP-GC)

Arab Nationalist Guards

Syrian Resistance (TSR)

Major Insurgent Umbrella Organisations

Moslem Brotherhood (MB)

Free Syrian Army

Syrian Islamic Front (IF)

Syrian Islamic Liberation Front (SILF)

Brigade of Islam/Army of Islam

Islamic Front (IF)

Major Insurgent Combat Units

Southern Front & Syria Revolutionaries Front (SRF)

Farouq Brigades

Grandsons of the Prophet Brigade

Islamic Movement of the Free Men of the Levant

Falcons of the Levant Brigade

Dawoud Brigade

Syrian Turkmen Brigades

Unity Brigade

Banner of the Nation Brigades

Army of Mujahedeen

Strangers of the Region of Syria

Jabahat an-Nusra (JAN)

The Green Battalion

Saraya Marwan Hadid

The Islamic State of Iraq and the Levant (ISIL/ISIS)

Northern Group/Jaysh al-Muharijeen wa al-Ansar (JMWA)

Lions of the Caliphate Battalion

Jamiat Jund ash-Sham

Jund Allah Brigade in Bilad ash-Sham

Syriac Military Council

A SyAAF Mi-8MT (serial number 1251) over Hama Province. As usual, the helicopter had its rear cargo doors open, for easier embarkation and disembarkation of 'passengers' – usually special forces operators. Notable is an indigenous chaff and flare dispenser installed under the boom and insignia of "The Works" – the SyAAF's major overhaul facility at Nayrab AB – in white below the cockpit (as per top sketch on page 2 of this colour section). (Photo by YoungHamwiLens, via R. S.)

Fighters of an Iraqi Shi'a militia taking away a Syrian insurgent captured during fighting in the southern suburbs of Damascus in November 2012. (via M.P.)

An Mi-25 (serial number 2802), operated by either the No. 765 or No. 766 Squadron from Bley AB (better known as Marj Ruhayyil in the West). After most of the fleet was overhauled in Russia in 2009 and 2010, it saw intensive combat deployment all over Syria from the second half of 2011, with small detachments of two to three helicopters regularly operating from Hmemeem, Afis, Abu ad-Duhor, Hama, Tha'leh, Dayr az-Zawr, Almazza and Khelkhleh, among others. (Syrian Ministry of Defence)

A platoon of three T-62Ms on the streets of the Bab Amr district in Homs in February 2012. (SNN)

This 'police'-marked BRDM-2 of the SyAA was knocked out together with at least one BMP-1 during an insurgent attack on a government checkpoint at Cairo Square in Homs in February 2012. (SNN)

Various insurgent groups active in Aleppo Province were reasonably well-equipped with heavy weaponry, like this 2S1 Gvozdika 122mm calibre self-propelled howitzer (operated by Harakat ash-Sham Brigade). However, the appearance of ISIS and the influence of foreign powers over them for much of 2013, meant that they were preoccupied fighting each other instead of the government or Islamic extremists.
(Harakat ash-Sham release)

A T-72 MBT of an unknown unit at the streets of Yabroud in March 2012. This town in the Qalamoun Range, overlooking the highway from Damascus to Homs, became a centrepiece of a large insurgent-controlled area during the first half of 2012. (via M.Z.)

A group of defectors from the SyAA, declaring their decision to join the FSA and insurgency, in Idlib Province in May 2012. Although usually armed only with AK-47s, and having few machine guns and RPG-7s, once free of tight control by superior military officers they proved quite successful in their early operations against government forces. (SNN)

and five captured in Idlib and Homs Provinces between 9 May and 16 June.

In early July, after squashing several huge demonstrations in the centre of Aleppo, elements of the 10th AD launched an offensive towards the north, in order to secure the roads to border crossings into Turkey, and land connections to the Minakh AB. This operation was not only beaten back with heavy loss, but resulted in additional mass defections and a situation where the insurgents were subsequently able to establish their first large units and bring sizeable swathes of this province under their control. Indeed, when the government rushed a big convoy supported by 23 armoured vehicles from Idlib in the direction of Aleppo, this was successively ambushed and nearly annihilated: by 26 June, it lost at least six T-55s and about a dozen BMP-1s, and the insurgents shot down a Mi-8 that attempted to provide support. Eventually, government forces in Aleppo Province were unable to continue offensive operations.

For all practical purposes, these were the last offensive operations of the Syrian Arab Army as such. Ever since, and with exception of battles for specific military bases, nearly all the offensive operations run on orders from the government in Damascus were undertaken by foreign combatants, sponsored by Iran, with only limited participation of the RGD and the 4th AD. Furthermore, it

became nearly impossible to distinguish what was left of the SyAA from various loyalist militias.

DAMASCUS VOLCANO

The security situation in much of Damascus remained critical despite government operations in March 2012. Large demonstrations held every day regularly resulted in violent attacks by military and intelligence operatives, and dozens were killed nearly every day. It was against this backdrop that the Syrian capital was hit by a series of powerful car bomb blasts that killed dozens and injured hundreds. While the opposition denied responsibility for most of these, the government insisted on accusing the then little-known Jabahat an-Nusra. Government claims that the majority of the population wanted stability and no government change was countered by general strikes that paralysed not only much of the capital but also Aleppo.

The FSA launched its first offensive inside Damascus on 20 May 2012, attacking checkpoints and military convoys in Kfar Souseh, Almazza, Malki and several other neighbourhoods, causing dozens of casualties. This provoked another spate of defections, which peaked four days later when a brigadier general and more than 200 officers and other ranks left their units and joined the insurgency, and on 21 June a disaffected Col Hassan Mirei al-Hamadeh defected with his MiG-21bis fighter from Khelkhleh AB to Jordan.

The military reacted by shelling many Damascus suburbs, but the FSA began attacking the military in the city centre and pro-government TV stations in the suburbs, and by the end of the month caused over 200 casualties in military personnel.[15]

The general chaos inside the Syrian capital eventually prompted insurgent commanders in the Damascus area – foremost Col Qassim Saadedine of the FSA – to start preparing a large-scale operation aimed at capturing the capital, codenamed 'Operation Damascus Volcano'. Precise details remain evasive, but it seems that Saadedine managed to concentrate up to 3,000 lightly armed fighters from different units allied with the FSA – including about 1,000 survivors of earlier fighting in Douma – and at least reasonable stocks of ammunition. However, his preparations were not only insufficient but were also revealed to the government, which ordered the Republican Guards Division into a pre-emptive attack against major insurgent concentrations in Midan and Tadhamon districts on 15 July. Although systematically encircling both areas and then driving special forces supported by T-72s and Mi-8 helicopter gunships into one neighbourhood after the other, the first attack on Midan was not successful. Among about 40 military and civilian officials killed was the Deputy Commander of Police in that district. Fighting in Tadamoun was as heavy, and eventually prompted the military to call for help from SyAAF Mi-8, Mi-17 and Mi-25 helicopter gunships. The FSA launched its offensive on 17 July, attacking from Kfar Sousa, Barzeh and Qaboun into the city centre, while simultaneously assaulting nearly all checkpoints in Rif Dimashq and cutting off the highways from Damascus to Dera'a and to Homs. On the next day, a suicide bomber demolished the National Security HQ in ar-Rawda district, killing the Minister of Defence Lt Gen Daoud Rajiha, Maj Gen Assef Shawkat and Lt Gen Hassan Turkmani (chief of Assad's Crisis Cell).[16] After insurgents overran Camp Sa'iqa in Basateen Almazza district, approached the Ministry of Defence, Parliament

Until June 2012, and in an attempt to create an image of 'regular forces fighting against Islamist extremist terrorist gangs', the Syrian government was regularly releasing details about at least some of its casualties. Once the popular uprising made the actual situation more than obvious, corresponding reporting all but ceased. This scene from a burrial of 23 SyAA officers and other ranks was photographed on 2 May 2012. (SANA)

The aftermath of one of many massacres committed by 'security forces' of the Syrian government on civilians in the Douma district of Damascus, in June 2012. Their burials were neither as flashy nor as celebrated as those of loyalist soldiers, and were nearly always interrupted by artillery or mortar attacks, sometimes even air strikes. (SNN via Y.A.)

Bashar al-Assad (right), swearing in Brig Gen Fahid Jasim al-Friej as a new Minister of Defence on 19 July 2012, following the assassination of Lt Gen Daoud Rajiha, Maj Gen Assef Shawkat and Lt Gen Hassan Turkmani two days earlier. (SANA)

Lengthy columns of sand-painted vehicles of the RGD became a regular sight on the streets of Damascus in late 2011, when this photograph of a T-72AV was taken. Of interest are storage boxes and part of the gun barrel painted in bright red, to differentiate tanks operated by loyalist forces from those operated by insurgents. This tank is showing scars of at least two RPG-attacks, both apparently deflected by ERA armour. (Photo by LensDimashqi, via M.Z.)

and the Central Bank, and ambushed a column of the 4th AD, destroying five T-72s and a BMP-1, Assad ordered whatever Army units were available from their bases around Damascus and along the Golan Heights straight into the capital.

By deploying the entire RGD, much of what was left of the 3rd AD and large parts of the 4th AD, the loyalists launched a major counteroffensive on 19 July. Preceded by heavy shelling and attacks by helicopter gunships, task forces composed of special forces and T-72 tanks successively forced the insurgents out of Midan, Tadhamon, Qaboun, Kfar Souseh, Jobar, Barzeh and Almazza.

This 'Battle of Damascus' was for all purposes over by 23 July, when most of the FSA-held districts inside the capital were overrun and the government declared that rebel forces were defeated. While providing a significant morale-booster for loyalist forces – which by that time began to show signs of tremendous fatigue after almost a year of fighting – and insurgents having suffered heavy losses, the fighting went on. By 1 August, the RGD and 4th AD were assaulting the Barzeh, Tadamoun and Hajar al-Aswad districts of Damascus, while the 3rd AD was attacking another insurgent stronghold in the town of al-Tal, outside the city. Eventually, heavy shelling and a series of massacres of the civilian

population forced the insurgents to withdraw from Damascus and al-Tal, but the heavy losses it had sustained by that time resulted in the military running out of steam while assaulting the suburbs of Darayya and Moadamiya, in late August, and these remaining under insurgent control ever since.[17]

ATTACK ON ALEPPO

Although usually said to have been under firm government control and to have seen only minimal protesting, parts of Aleppo have seen significant demonstrations and violence since April 2011. Insurgent groups became active within the outskirts of the city during the spring of 2012, and conducted numerous attacks on military bases between April and June. The government reacted by cutting off all public services to districts where demonstrations took place, but this decision back-fired massively. The insurgency spread even faster in the countryside around Aleppo and when parts of the 78th Armoured Brigade attempted to attack protesters in Azzaz, 30km north-west of Aleppo, on 11 July, the FSA easily beat the assault back, destroying and capturing a number of T-72s in the process. Eight days later, Azzaz was completely liberated as several thousand insurgents from 18 different groups launched an advance into northern and eastern Aleppo, where they joined local militias. Confronted by this onslaught, remnants of the 56th Brigade – with the addition of cadres from the former 18th and 85th Mechanised Brigades – deployed in a semi-circle around the biggest city in Syria, stretching from Anadan, Tel Rifaat, via Minakh AB and Azzaz to al-Bab, fell back into Aleppo, leaving behind significant amounts of heavy arms, ammunition and supplies. By 21 July, the insurgents had advanced deep into the city, bringing the Haydariya, Sakhour and Sallahaddin Districts under control, before continuing into Saif ad-Dawla and al-Jameeliya towards the Old City and medieval citadel, which are a United Nations World Heritage site. Local counterattacks by the T-72-equipped battalion of the 56th Brigade were slow, hesitant and followed the typical conduct of operations by government forces during the first two years of the conflict: small groups of tanks moved up and down major streets, expecting the opposition to flee at their sight. Considering that most insurgent units were led by former officers of Syrian special forces, it was unsurprising that most such probes were ambushed and largely destroyed on 22 and 23 July. As several other Army units collapsed due to defections, the first major battle inside Aleppo developed only when the opposition reached the city's main intelligence headquarters, where the AFI and SSI operatives managed to stop them. Redirecting their advance, the insurgents launched an attack into the Old City, and after securing it continued to push westwards, claiming to have shot down two helicopters and destroyed at least six armoured vehicles on 24 July.

Alerted by the crisis in Aleppo, the government in Damascus once again reacted by scrambling reinforcements from all over the country. Units stationed in western Aleppo – like the cadre of the Artillery School, combined with remnants of the 56th, 18th and 85th Brigades, and the 80th Artillery Regiment – were ordered to slow down the enemy advance by bombarding all districts controlled by insurgents. Meanwhile, practically all the remaining Army units were withdrawn from northern and north-eastern Syria – mainly from Kurdish regions, where only small forces were left behind in Qamishly to protect local bases and key oil and gas infrastructure. Several additional companies from the 3rd, 4th, 10th, 11th, 17th and 18th Divisions, and most of the 416th SF Regiment (established from Alawite reservists in the Tartous area and trained by Iranian instructors in early 2012), were rushed from Hama, Homs and the Mediterranean coast. They were followed by troops drawn from a number of air defence units previously stationed in northern and north-eastern Syria, which were ordered to abandon their SAM sites and reorganised as infantry formations. As usual, once in the Aleppo area, all the various elements were reorganised, with companies from the 4th AD being combined with elements of various other units to create between eight and ten new, battalion-sized 'task forces'. For example, one such task force consisted of a mechanised company from the 4th AD, combined with a company each from the 416th SF Regiment, a company from the 56th AB and one artillery battery from the Artillery School.

In this fashion, the government managed to concentrate around 20,000 troops, which were deployed for the first large-scale counterattack into the Sallahaddin, Fardous and Ansari Districts on the afternoon of 28 July. Although preceded by nearly eight hours of artillery bombardment and air strikes, the attack was beaten back with some loss. The insurgents in Aleppo operated in a different fashion to elsewhere in Syria. They would deploy their snipers on rooftops to knock out government snipers. After that, the same snipers would start to target government infantry, separating it from the armour. Left on its own, the T-72 and T-62 tanks of Army units were easy pickings for RGP-7-armed insurgents.

The government restarted its counterattack after the arrival of

The 78th Armoured Brigade suffered heavy losses while rushing into Aleppo in response to a surprise insurgent advance on the city in late July and early August 2012. These two T-72s belonged to a company that was decimated within 10 minutes on the early morning of 3 August 2012. (SNN)

This column of BMP-1s and support vehicles of the Army made the deadly mistake of driving into a narrow alley in the outskirts of southern Aleppo, the exit of which was blocked by an earthen barricade. All vehicles were quickly destroyed by insurgents, with a heavy loss of crews, on 27 July 2012. (SNN)

During their advance on Aleppo, the insurgents had overrun the town of Andan, capturing or destroying the entire complement of T-55s from the 88th Brigade in the process on 31 July 2012. These two MBTs were rapidly camouflaged in order to conceal them from prying eyes of SyAAF L-39 pilots. (SNN)

Two T-72AVs of the 4th AD in the outskirts of south-western Aleppo in August 2012. (via M.Z..)

A T-72AV and troops of the 104th Brigade RGD during an advance into the Old City of Aleppo in mid-August 2012. (via M.Z.)

the 104th Mechanised Brigade RGD, and this time a well-co-ordinated operation of mechanised infantry, special forces and T-72 tanks resulted in the recovery of the ancient citadel and some parts of the Old City two days later. On 8 August, the 104th Brigade managed to breach insurgent positions and concentrate about a dozen of tanks on one of the crucial roundabouts in the Sallahaddin district. Having a free field of fire, this small force held out until the evening, when it was reinforced by infantry and intelligence operatives, which secured five streets. However, an insurgent counterattack recovered three of these on the next day.

Following several days of artillery shelling and sustained air strikes, on 12 August the government attacked into the western Saif ad-Dawla and Sukari Districts, but was finally stopped cold when the insurgents managed to resupply their forces with ammunition. Already exhausted from months of intensive operations, government forces in Aleppo subsequently ran out of steam. Although having only around 8,000 combatants who were short on ammunition and supplies, and despite considerable losses, the

insurgents fought back bitterly and managed to retain most of the positions they had reached during their initial advance. With government troops critically short on fuel, tanks and troops, and insurgents lacking firepower and supplies, since late August 2012 the fighting in Aleppo has degenerated into a long and very exhausting battle of attrition.

5
AIR FORCE TO THE RESCUE

During the first year of the conflict, government forces were relatively successful in clearing most important parts of all the major urban centres – which was necessary for Bashar al-Assad's survival and legitimacy of maintaining himself in power – but then remained in place to hold what they secured. Simultaneously, unable to recruit and retain enough forces to control all of Syria, the government lost most of the countryside. Furthermore, after securing Damascus, Homs and Idlib, it literally ran out of fuel necessary to manoeuvre large forces. This short-sighted policy resulted in a number of additional mistakes. Actively seeking to force civilians out of insurgent-held areas and to clear insurgents out of population centres, government forces launched a campaign of brutal ethnic cleansing and displacement of large parts of the population with the help of artillery, air strikes and periodic massacres, in turn pushing thousands of men into the hands of the insurgency and provoking a sectarian civil war.

Ironically, while proving increasingly unable to control the resulting conflict, out of concern about a possible Western intervention, Damascus kept a significant part of its military strength – the Syrian Arab Air Forces – back, deploying it extremely cautiously during the first 16 months of protesting

One of many T-62s knocked out by insurgents during repeated attacks on ar-Rastan in June and July 2012 – all of which were beaten back with extensive losses (including more than 40 MBTs and IFVs) for loyalists. Expecting the insurgents to run away upon seeing them, loyalist commanders repeatedly deployed their armour without sufficient infantry and artillery support into densely built-up areas, with unavoidable results. (via M.Z.)

and then insurgency. Mi-8 and Mi-17 helicopters were used to transport special forces into attacks on protesters and – later on – haul reinforcements and supplies to isolated bases. Sporadically, Mi-25 helicopter gunships were deployed to disperse larger protests or attack early insurgent concentrations. Fighter-bombers – primarily lighter types like MiG-21s – flew very few attacks on well-defended targets in Homs and Rastan during the first half of 2012. It took large-scale insurgent attacks into Damascus, Dayr az-Zawr and then Aleppo for the government to gradually intensify deployment of air power, and then a series of painful defeats through autumn 2012 for Bahsar to order the SyAAF into all-out operations.

SYRIAN ARAB AIR FORCES AND AIR DEFENCE

Internally known as the 'silent service', the Syrian Arab Air Forces (SyAAF) was and remains the core support base of the Syrian government. Hafez al-Assad became politically active after flying Gloster Meteors in the 1950s, and MiG-15s and MiG-17s in the early 1960s.[18] He established his original power base while serving as a base commander and climbed to power in Damascus while acting as the Commander of the SyAAF and later on Minister of Defence. It was under his command that the AFI became the most powerful (and notorious) intelligence agency and internal security service in the country.

Contrary to intelligence services and military branches closely tied to the government, the SyAAF was not dominated by Alawites, but by Sunnis. However, whether serving in the SyAAF or in any of the related branches or intelligence departments, its officers and NCOs were always hand-picked for their loyalty, pampered with better pay and other incentives and privileges. They remained the most closely monitored part of the Syrian armed forces: any kind of dissent among pilots usually resulted in re-assignment to specific units – primarily those flying MiG-23BNs – renowed for being 'spent' in combat if and when required. Contrary to the usual expectations, the SyAAF thus has shown an absolute

minimum of dissent since the start of unrest in Syria. In two years of war, the SyAAF has lost fewer officers to desertion – only about a dozen active pilots and several mid-ranking officers – than the AFI. This is one of the biggest surprises of this conflict, even more so because through all this time specific squadron commanders (and their deputies) were receiving operational orders not from their superiors, but from the Ba'ath Party HQ in Damascus.

Irrespective of operating obsolete aircraft, and despite many foreign assessments supposing 'historical maintenance issues', the SyAAF as of 2011 was a small, yet compact, well-trained and well-maintained force. Supported by 'The Factory' – a major overhaul facility, capable of maintaining all aircraft and helicopters in service – at Nayrab AB (Aleppo IAP), it had a well-developed maintenance infrastructure capable of local overhauls and upgrades of all available combat aircraft and helicopters, and of manufacturing spare parts. Additional spare parts – often including entire assemblies – were acquired from Belarus and Ukraine during the 1990s and 2000s. Nevertheless, the SyAAF did experience a lengthy period of neglect by the government during that time, and as of 2010–2011 was in the process of overhauling and reconditioning most of its aircraft and helicopters. While most of the corresponding work was undertaken at home, types like Mi-25s and Su-24MKs were overhauled and upgraded in Russia.

As of 2011, the SyAAF was under the command of Maj Gen Isam Hallak (hero of the 1973 war with Israel, but replaced by Maj Gen Ahmad Balloul a year later). It used to have 13 squadrons of combat aircraft, 14 squadrons of helicopters and three transport units organised into three (alpha-numerically-designated) operational divisions, and the training command.[19] Nominally, each fighter/fighter-bomber squadron and each helicopter squadron should have operated 12 aircraft, but some units were under-strength, while others – like the Su-24-equipped No. 819 Squadron – operated additional equipment. Details about organisation and equipment of the SyAAF as of 2011–2013 are provided in Tables 2 and 3.

Table 2:
SyAAF Order of Battle, 2011–2013

Unit	Base	Equipment	Remarks
Training Command			
Basic Flight School	Minakh AB	SIAT 223K-1	School closed in May 2012; personnel and aircraft re-distributed to other units in Aleppo Province; base overrun by insurgents in August 2013
Basic Flight School	Minakh AB	Mi-2, Mi-8	School closed in May 2012; personnel and aircraft re-distributed to other units in Aleppo Province; base overrun by insurgents in August 2013
The Factory	Nayrab AB		Major aircraft overhaul facility; base under siege by insurgents from October 2012 until April 2013
Advanced Flight School	Kweres AB	L-39ZA/ZO	Base known as Rasin el-Aboud in the West; School closed in May 2012; base under siege by insurgents from November 2012 until March 2014
Jet Flying School	Ksheesh	L-39ZA/ZO	Base known as Jirrah in the West; School closed in May 2012; overrun by insurgents in April 2013, with 14 L-39s captured (2 operational, 2 under maintenance and 10 stored)
(Northern) Air Division			
	Afis AB	Mi-8	Base (also known as Taftanaz) overrun by insurgents, with 15 Mi-8 helicopters from 253 and 257 Squadrons destroyed or abandoned
	Tabqa AB	L-39ZA/ZO	Base under siege by insurgents; former No.12 Squadron (MiG-21MFs) was disbanded before the war; few L-39s and MiG-21s now stationed there

	Abu ad-Duhor AB		Base overrun by insurgents in November 2012; returned to government control in 2013 and used by helicopters, but under siege again
2/253/257 Squadron	ar-Raqqa Airport	Mi-8	6–8 survivors from Afis and Minakh moved to this airport
8 Squadron	Dayr az-Zawr AB	MiG-21bis/UM Mi-25 & Mi-8	Base under siege by insurgents from July 2012 until May 2013; only 4 MiG-21s operational as of late 2013; few Mi-25s, Mi-8s and MiG-23BNs forward deployed occasionally
679 Squadron	Hamah AB	MiG-21bis/UM	Unit very active over Idlib Province; few missions over Aleppo Province as well
680 'Tiger' Squadron	Hamah AB	MiG-21bis/UM	Unit very active over Idlib and Hamah Provinces; CO Col Ammar defected in December 2012
(Central) Air Division			
	Dhab'ah AB		Base known as al-Qusayr AB in the West; closed in 2009 and used for delivery of Iranian weapons for Hezbollah; overrun by insurgents in April 2013 but recaptured in June 2013
675 Squadron	Sh'eirat AB	MiG-23ML/UM	7–9 operational aircraft
677 Squadron	Sh'eirat AB	Su-22M-3K	8–9 operational aircraft
685 Squadron	Sh'eirat AB	Su-22M-4K	7–8 operational aircraft
819 Squadron	T-4/Tiyas AB	Su-24MK	12–15 operational aircraft, all meanwhile overhauled and upgraded
827 Squadron	T-4/Tiyas AB	Su-22M-4K	7–8 operational aircraft
7 Squadron	T-4/Tiyas AB	MiG-25RB	2 aircraft returned to service in 2011 (rest of fleet deactivated in 2009)
?? Squadron	Tadmor	Mi-17	Base also known as Palmyra in the West
618 Squadron	Hmemeem AB	Mi-14	Bassel el-Assad/Lattakiya IAP; only Mi-14 are known to be operational; some Ka-25s are undergoing overhauls but status presently unknown
(Southern) Air Division			
695 Squadron	An-Nassiriya	MiG-23BN	7–8 operational aircraft
698 Squadron	An-Nassiriya	MiG-23BN	7–8 operational aircraft
697 Squadron	As-Seen AB	MiG-29	Base known as Tsaykal AB in the West; presently, 12–15 operational aircraft
?? Squadron	Dmeyr AB	Su-22M-3K	6–7 operational aircraft
54 Squadron	Dmeyr AB	MiG-23ML	9–10 operational aircraft
976/977 Squadron	Almazza	SA.342 Gazelle	Helicopters stored, seldom flown
?? Squadron	Almazza	Mi-8 & Mi-25	Unknown unit present since late 2012, including at least 3 Mi-25s
	Marj as-Sultan		Base overrun by insurgents in early January 2012; 525/537/909 Squadrons disbanded or now based at Almazza
945 Squadron	Khelkhleh	MiG-21bis	
946 Squadron	Khelkhleh	MiG-21bis	
765 Squadron	Blei AB	Mi-25	Detachments at Almazza, Khelkhleh and Suwayda
766 Squadron	Blei AB	Mi-25	Detachments at Hmemeem, Hama, and Dayr az-Zawr
	Tha'leh AB		Base known as Suwayda in the West; no permanently attached units but used for regular deployments of Mi-8s and Mi-25s
522 Squadron	Damascus IAP	An-26, Il-76M	1 Il-76 abandoned at Abu ad-Duhor (October 2012); only 3–4 aircraft remain operational
565 Squadron	Damascus IAP	Yak-40	Only 3–4 aircraft operational (one written off due to damage by ground fire at Dayr az-Zawr)
575 Squadron	Damascus IAP	Falcon 20E, Falcon 900	VIP transport unit
532 Squadron	Set Zeinab AB	Mi-8	Base known as Qabr as-Sitt in the West

Table 3:
Major Aircraft Types of the SyAAF, 2011

Aircraft/Helicopter Type	Number of available airframes & Remarks
Mi-8/17	150 available; some 20 undergoing overhauls in Syria
Mi-25	22 available; at least 3 still undergoing overhauls in Russia[20]
Mi-14	12–14 available, only 5–6 operational
L-39	50 available
MiG-21bis	60 available; 30 additional aircraft in storage
MiG-23BN (fighter-bombers only)	40–50 available; 30 additional aircraft in storage
MiG-23MF/ML/MLD	30 available; 20 additional aircraft in storage
MiG-25 (all variants)	None operational, 2 MiG-25R reconnaissance fighters returned to service
MiG-29	20 available, 12–15 undergoing overhauls
Su-22M-3/4K	30–40 available
Su-24M	21 available, 12–15 undergoing overhauls (some in Russia)
Transports	10–12 available, including An-26, Il-76, Yak-40, but some stored

The Sh'eirat-based No. 677 Squadron and an unknown unit based at Dmeyr AB are still operating about 20 Su-22M-3Ks. This classic, swing-wing design of the 1970s proved a true workhorse, capable of lifting up to 3,000kg of bombs and flying most combat sorties of the Syrian Civil War. (Photo by R.S.)

Although interceptor types like the MiG-21bis, MiG-23MF/ML and the MiG-29 used to play the most important role within the SyAAF over past decades, recently overhauled and upgraded Su-24MK fighter-bombers like this example (serial number 3508) have been flying most air strikes against insurgent strongholds since mid-2012. (Syrian Ministry of Defence)

Less numerous than Su-22M-3Ks and Su-22M-4Ks, the SyAAF's MiG-23BN proved to have a longer range than the Sukhoi design, and were thus used to strike targets in distant areas, primarily around Dayr az-Zawr, during the summer of 2012, being intensively deployed in the Damascus area for the rest of that year. This example (apparently serialled as 1679) was photographed while releasing two FAB-500M-62 general-purpose bombs over Rif Dimashq in autumn 2012. (via R.S.)

An Mi-8T armed with four UV-16-57 rocket pods in flight over the town of Azzaz on 25 July 2012. After falling under insurgent control two days later, Azzaz was subjected to several ground attacks and then a campaign of terrible bombardment by the SyAAF, which killed hundreds of civilians. (via R.S.)

The once mighty Air Defence Force (ADF) suffered heavily due to negligence and lack of funding during the 1990s and 2000s. Established as a separate branch of the Syrian military in the spring of 1973 (during preparations for the October 1973 war with Israel), it was re-assigned to the SyAAF as the Air Defence Directorate in 2011.[21] At the peak of its strength, in the late 1980s, this command consisted of about 35 air defence brigades, each including at least four, some as many as six SAM battalions (each battalion operated one SAM site), and a well-developed early warning radar network that used to be one of the most advanced in the Middle East. As such, the ADF exercised operational control over ground-based air defences and manned interceptors nominally assigned to the SyAAF.

What was left of this force in 2011 was still organised into one air defence division, supervising six air defence zones that covered the entire territory of Syria.[22] Because of the withdrawal from service of older systems – like SA-2s (S-75 Dvina) and SA-5s (S-200 Volga) – and block obsolescence of such systems as SA-3 (S-125 Pechora) and SA-6 (3M9 Kvadrat), the number of operational brigades was more than halved. However, with help of Iranian financial support, the reorganised Air Defence Directorate (ADD) received not only a much leaner organisational structure, but was also much better equipped. Since 2008, Syria has purchased eight SA-17 Grizzly (Buk-M2E) batteries, and about 20 SA-22 (Pantsyr-1S) systems from Russia. Furthermore, some of the SA-3 sites were upgraded to Pechora-2T standard with components purchased from Belarus, while most of the remaining SA-6 sites were upgraded through the integration of SA-11 (Kub-M4) systems.

The ADD experienced the same spate of defections as the Army in 2011, and several of its battalions were subsequently deployed as infantry (usually corseted by intelligence services).

GRADUAL ESCALATION

The SyAAF participation in the civil war experienced a gradual escalation. Deployment of helicopters for transport purposes dominated in 2011, but its role intensified through early 2012, when attacks on neighbourhoods, towns and villages controlled by insurgents became as common as resupply flights for garrisons isolated by insurgent advances. Correspondingly, the first losses

A heavily fortified air defence complex, including one SA-2 site protecting Damascus IAP, as seen in 2009. The ADD suffered a spate of defections in 2011 and 2012, dozens of SAM and radar sites were overrun by insurgents, while others were transformed into artillery bases for loyalists, and some of its units were relegated to infantry duties. (Photo by Tom Cooper)

A rare photograph taken in May 2013 of a TELAR belonging to eight SA-17 Grizzly batteries operated by the Air Defence Directorate (ADD) of the SyAAF (launch rails installed at the top of the vehicle are covered by tarpaulin). Most such systems are concentrated in the Damascus area, but a few are protecting vital installations along the coast. Their presence did not prevent the Israeli Air and Space Force from launching a number of stand-off attacks against selected targets inside Syria in 2012 and 2013. (via M.Z.)

the SyAAF suffered during this war were all related to Mi-8 and Mi-17 helicopters. Interestingly, the relatively large fleet of French-built Aérospatiale SA.342 Gazelle light helicopters was deployed only sparingly, primarily over the Dera'a Province in spring and summer 2011, and has hardly ever been seen since.

Meanwhile, other units were undergoing an intensive process of overhauling and upgrading their aircraft, obviously preparing for 'the inevitable'. Most of the surviving Mi-25 helicopter gunships were overhauled in Russia, followed by the entire SyAAF fleet of 21 Su-24MK fighter-bombers (upgraded to Su-24MK2 standard at the 514 ARZ plant in Rzhev).[23] Similarly, most of the remaining MiG-29s were brought to MiG-29M2 standard at "The Works" at Nayrab AB, with the help of assemblies delivered from Russia.

'The inevitable' finally came in the summer of 2012, when Damascus, Aleppo and Dayr az-Zawr came under a near simultaneous assault. Already in a state of chaos from the scattered deployment of its major units (necessary in order to prevent unit-level defections), and overstretched because of the need to maintain a presence in all of Syria, the government found itself in a situation where it lacked the troop strength and firepower to drive insurgents out of major urban centres. Its armour and indirect fire proved unable to stop insurgent advances, and because of this the SyAAF was ordered into action.

The first area to see intensive aerial strikes was Dayr az-Zawr. A series of defections of top AFI officers and military commanders resulted in the near collapse of local security structures and

emergence of several large insurgent formations between 20 July and 3 August 2012.[24] The SyAAF deployed MiG-23BNs and Su-24MKs to bomb suspected insurgent concentrations and HQs on 24 July, but these primarily hit private homes, killing scores of civilians. With family and tribal ties being particularly strong in this part of Syria, the bombardments caused ever more outrage and most of the defectors joined the insurgency. With the help of intelligence they provided, the Qaqaa Brigade attacked and destroyed the HQ of the Political Security Branch in the city, together with several armoured vehicles deployed for its protection, on 8 August. With the help of captured weapons, additional insurgent units came into being, including the Otham Ibn Affan Battalion of the Ahfad Muhammad Brigades, which created a number of 'technicals' by installing heavy machine guns of 14.7mm calibre on the rear platform of their 4WDs. During the following days this unit began setting up ambushes for SyAAF fighter bombers which, expecting no serious resistance, continuously operated at low altitudes. On 13 August, a MiG-23BN flown by Col Mohammad Suleiman attacked Mohasan, a village outside Dayr az-Zawr, and was hit by machine gun fire. The pilot ejected and was captured shortly afterwards. The insurgency thus scored its first confirmed claim for a SyAAF fighter bomber in the war.

The SyAAF's freedom of operation over north-eastern Syria further deteriorated when insurgents overran the garrison of al-Bukamal, a town on the Euphrates river some 110km south-east of Dayr az-Zawr, on the opposite side of the border from the Iraqi town of al-Qaim, later in August. It was here that the first stocks of Russian-made SA-7 MANPADs were captured. It is therefore unsurprising that it was in north-eastern Syria where the SyAAF lost its first Su-22 (and its pilot) on 5 September.

Meanwhile, the SyAAF began deploying Su-22s to hit densely populated quarters in Anadan, Azzaz and al-Bab, attempting to punish the local population for supporting the uprising, while Su-24s began bombing local military bases that were overrun by insurgents in order to destroy extensive stocks of ammunition and supplies abandoned there. Mi-8 and Mi-25 helicopters and L-39 light strikers were providing support for loyalist troops encircled at Minakh AB. Azzaz was particularly heavily hit by four Su-22s on 15 August, when dozens of civilians were killed.

The situation inside Aleppo proved more problematic – for both sides. With help from a well-developed network of informers, the SyAAF experienced few problems in tracking and finding major insurgent concentrations, headquarters and bases. However, the presence of lots of foreign journalists made Damascus reluctant

A SyAAF L-39 light striker pulling up from an attack on south-eastern Aleppo in mid-September 2012. Throughout the first four months of the war, at least two L-39s from either Kweres or Ksheesh ABs were airborne over the city throughout every single day. (via R.S.)

Most Il-76 transports of the SyAAF are wearing SyrianAir markings, like the example here, registered as YK-ATB and photographed in the 1980s. The fleet had spent much of the 2000s grounded at Damascus IAP, but was in the process of reactivation at the start of the war and has seen heavy use ever since. (Joe Dede Collection)

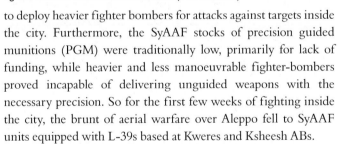

A sequence of stills showing the downing of a MiG-23BN flown by Col Suleiman over Mohasan on 13 August 2012. This was the first SyAAF fighter-bomber shot down in the war. (FSA release)

An SyAAF Mi-8 armed with what appears to be two FAB-100-120 bombs on inboard pylons, photographed while low over the Sakhur district of Aleppo in late August 2012. (via R.S.)

to deploy heavier fighter bombers for attacks against targets inside the city. Furthermore, the SyAAF stocks of precision guided munitions (PGM) were traditionally low, primarily for lack of funding, while heavier and less manoeuvrable fighter-bombers proved incapable of delivering unguided weapons with the necessary precision. So for the first few weeks of fighting inside the city, the brunt of aerial warfare over Aleppo fell to SyAAF units equipped with L-39s based at Kweres and Ksheesh ABs.

Like in Dayr az-Zawr and around Aleppo, L-39-pilots primarily attempted to bomb insurgent HQs and bases, but they flew even more punitive attacks, targeting bakeries and hospitals. During late July and early August, they encountered next to no resistance because the opposition not only lacked suitable weapons, but also training and practice in engaging fast jets. Therefore the L-39s – which usually operated in pairs – were free to roam the skies as they wanted. Between 18 and 21 August, for example, they hit the same insurgent HQ inside Aleppo no less but four times, while Mi-8s and Mi-25s heavily bombed the Sallahaddin, Saif ad-Dawla, and Soleimaniyah Districts. During this period, Nayrab AB/Aleppo IAP was still secure enough to permit landings of Ilyushin Il-76 transports, which brought much needed supplies and reinforcements. The situation changed after the opposition overran Camp Hanano in the north-eastern outskirts of the city on 7 September, capturing not only additional stocks of ammunition but also a small number of SA-7s.

The month of August saw the first SyAAF interventions on a number of other battlefields around the Idlib Province. On 14 August, the government deployed a convoy consisting of companies from several mechanised units from Idlib in the direction of the Bab al-Hawa crossing on the Turkish border. This site had been captured by insurgents of the Dera'a al-Thawra Brigade in May, but abandoned on Turkish insistence. It was re-captured in mid-July, but by then the military had constructed a strongly-fortified position within the old border crossing a few kilometres away. The 30km journey from Idlib to Bab al-Hawa proved arduous for the loyalists, their column being ambushed three times – in M'arat Misrin, Hazano and Batbo – losing vehicles and personnel before having to stop. On the next morning, the garrison in Bab al-Hawa launched a break-out attempt, dashing in the direction of Idlib. This column was ambushed too, losing armoured vehicles, trucks and troops. Eventually, only a bedazzled collection of about 500 survivors reached Idlib, leaving behind at least three T-55s, one T-72M1, one ARV armoured engineering vehicle, three BMP-1s, one BTR-60 or BRDM, one armoured truck on a LandCruiser chassis and about a dozen other vehicles all destroyed, over 100 casualties, and two T-55s, two T-72s and one T-62 abandoned, along with plenty of equipment and ammunition.[25] Thanks to captured weaponry, the insurgents subsequently assaulted a number of government strongpoints around Ariha and Jabal az-

Zawiya, causing additional heavy losses in men and materiel. After this fiasco, the leadership of the Ba'ath Party issued a direct order to the HQ of SyAAF in Damascus and units based at Hama AB to launch an indiscriminate bombing campaign against the outskirts of Idlib and nearby villages, Ariha, Jabal az-Zawiya, Ma'arat an-Numaan and several other towns. These attacks were to punish the local population for their resistance and to drive it out of the area.

In mid-August, the SyAAF also become involved in fighting in Damascus, Rif Dimashq and Homs Provinces. Rastan and Talbiseh were subjected to heavy strikes by Mi-25s and MiG-21s, but after local insurgents obtained a number of SA-7s, the SyAAF introduced the practice of only deploying high-flying Su-22s and Su-24s over this area. Further south, on 15 August, the entire 2nd Battalion of the 55th Brigade ADF, based in Dmeyr, defected to the insurgent side, prompting the SyAAF to order Su-22s and MiG-23MFs from the nearby air base to bomb that town too, without regard for the families of involved pilots and ground personnel. Obviously, this caused great consternation and even some resistance within the ranks of the air force, but any dissent was kept under control by the AFI and repeated orders from the Ba'ath Party – which appealed to its members within operational squadrons of the SyAAF, expecting them to 'lead by example'.[26]

SEEDS OF RIFT

Due to continuous defections from the military, the FSA reached a nominal strength of about 60,000 combatants between June and August 2012, organised in about 80 battalions, some of which began specialising in tasks like logistics, transport or medical support. Its command structure remained decentralised: the small cadre of top officers was evacuated to Turkey, which offered some support but nowhere near what the insurgents expected. The failure of the offensive on Damascus, stalemate in Aleppo and pressure from foreign powers began causing a number of rifts within the insurgency during the summer of 2012.

Because it was established as an apolitical and non-religious organisation, and insisted on toppling the government before leaving it to the Syrian population to decide what form of government and religious order it would have in the future, the FSA found itself on the receiving end of much pressure from abroad. While the position of officers that established the organisation was unsurprising for Syrians – who in the last 60 years never got a chance to learn to think about the future beyond the end of the current month – it was unthinkable for most of its potential foreign supporters: they insisted the FSA subject itself to various political and religious ideals. The Turkish government of Premier Minister Recep Tayyip Erdogan began imposing ultimatums upon the FSA leaders to accept the leadership of the Moslem Brotherhood as early as November 2011. The officers around Riyahd al-Assad first refused to obey, but eventually agreed to co-ordinate their activities with civilians of the Syrian National Council (SNC). This coalition of about 140 oppositional figures – some 90 of whom were living outside Syria – primarily included members of the Moslem Brotherhood, but also a few Kurds, Assyrians and others, and was based in Istanbul, Turkey. For the reasons described above, not only the FSA, but the majority of activists and various ethnic and tribal leaders had no affiliations with such, 'older' political ideologies like those of the

Brotherhood. Most of them could neither understand nor accept the leadership of a group of politicians unknown to them.

With Western powers succumbing to the government's PR-campaign, and those run by its foreign supporters, about all insurgents being 'Islamic extremists', and restraining from getting involved, official – but mostly unofficial and usually private – efforts of various interest groups from abroad resulted in the appearance of a number of splinter groups, usually led by civilians or low-ranking defectors with undeniable ideological – primarily Islamist – motivation. Following the Turkish example, official and unofficial 'interest groups' from Saudi Arabia, Qatar and Kuwait began to search for ways of establishing themselves in control over different parts of the insurgency.

During the summer of 2012, the Turkey-supported Moslem Brotherhood began channelling the majority of funds to selected Islamist groups nominally under the control of the FSA. Some large insurgent formations – primarily the Idlib-based Suqour ash-Sham Brigade – complained bitterly, but to no avail. The ideals of the FSA attracted mainly Sunnis, many of whom were religiously conservative. While they did not consider themselves any kind of 'Mujahidin' or stereotypical Islamic extremists, and their general goals were secular, Islam provided them with inspiration and strength. Nevertheless, under pressure from abroad, some groups soon began superimposing Islamic ideals for little else but satisfaction of their foreign donors. Over time this became the norm, resulting in ever better financing that enabled a number of insurgent units that used to pledge allegiance to the FSA to grow and became capable of operating in multiple provinces, entirely independently from its supposed leadership. This was an opportunity eagerly exploited by not a few outside powers-to-be.

Suqour ash-Sham thus became one of the first major insurgent units operating independently from the FSA. During August 2012, a large part of the insurgent units operational in Damascus followed its pattern and grouped within what became known as the Syrian Islamic Liberation Front (Jabhat Tahrir Suriya al-Islamiyyah, SILF), developing one of the strongest armed coalitions in Syria by the end of the year. Foreign donors in Arab countries along the Persian Gulf reacted by bolstering their support for this new organisation, eventually making it powerful enough to bring the districts of Darayya, Hajar al-Aswad and Moadamiyeh under its control by 22 August, and launch several attacks on the major government stronghold at Almazza AB. When the fighting spread along the highway to Damascus IAP towards the south, Arbeen, Jobar, Kfar Souseh and Zamalka came under insurgent control too, and the government reacted by deploying the RGD and intelligence operatives in a brutal attack into Kfar Souseh. Supported by Mi-8/17 helicopter gunships and MiG-21s from Khelkhleh AB, this succeeded in pushing out the insurgents but was primarily marked by widespread summary executions of hundreds of civilians.

Meanwhile, Saudi Arabia opened negotiations with various emerging factions, attempting to establish an organised structure with a well-defined chain of command, including experienced and authoritative officers with legitimacy from earlier combat against government forces. However, the authority of the emerging 'Joint Command' was nearly instantly undermined by a Qatari decision to focus upon aiding regional Military Councils directly, instead of down the chain of command, to which the Saudis reacted by exercising direct control over the top, and appointing their own favourites in command of areas where they previously exercised no influence. In turn, this angered many insurgents who felt that the new leadership had been forced upon them, and preferred to elect their own leaders. Eventually, this resulted in the emergence of two functioning Military Council leaders in most parts of Syria, together with all the related rivalry and infighting. Only partially solved through the creation of the Supreme Military Council (SMC) in November 2012 – officially a military body operating on behalf of the Syrian Opposition Coalition, with Brig Gen Salim Idriss as the most prominent representative – the rivalry between the Saudis and Qataris remains a dominant issue and the primary reason for the factionalisation of the insurgency ever since, coupled with a surge in religiosity and sectarianism. Following the example of the Suqour ash-Sham Brigade, the Farouq Brigade in Homs declared itself independent from the FSA, while Syrian Salafists began organising themselves into groups like the Islamic Movement of the Free Men of the Levant (Harakat Ahrar ash-

This BMP-1 was captured by insurgents of the Dawn of Islam Brigades (which is what the inscription on its side is citing) in Ma'arat an-Numaan, when the town was definitely brought under their control in September 2012. Like so many other insurgent units, the Dawn of Islam pledged alliance with the FSA early on, only to join one of the umbrella organisations with Islamist ideology at a later date. (via Y.A.)

The war in Syria resulted in the widespread proliferation of so-called 'technicals' on both sides of the conflict. This Toyota truck was modified through the installation of a ZU-23 flak cannon of 23mm calibre on its flat bed while operated by one of the insurgent units active in the Aleppo area and allied with the Syrian Islamic Liberation Front, and later the Islamic Front, during the second half of 2012. Except for air defence purposes, such weapons are primarily used for ground warfare. (IF)

Sham al-Islami), and the Support Front for the People of Levant by the Levantine Mujaheddin on the Battlefields of Jihad (Jabhat an-Nusra il-Ahl ash-Sham min Mujahedi ash-Sham fi Sahat al-Jihad, usually shortened to an-Nusra Front, Jabhat an-Nusra, or JAN). Finally, dozens, then hundreds and finally thousands of Jihadists from abroad began entering Syria, where most of them joined the Wahhabist 'Islamic State of Iraq and ash-Sham' (ISIS). The co-operation between the JAN and ISIS resulted in most other insurgent groups in northern and north-eastern Syria being marginalised by mid-2013.

It was under these circumstances that – because of general chaos and lack of funding, equipment and means of communications – the FSA lost control over large parts of the insurgency. Unknown at the time, it was to forever remain an idea, a catch-all brand referring to armed opposition in Syria in general. Although dozens of battalions and – later on – many powerful brigades and then provincial Military Councils continued declaring their allegiance to the organisation, the FSA never became even a franchise, and certainly not a coherent organisation with a clear, unified command structure, exercising control over operations in all of Syria. Worse still, as subsequent developments were to show, this series of events from the summer of 2012 was to signal the end of the revolution and genuine insurgency against the government of Bashar al-Assad, and the start of a Civil War, which eventually conflagrated into a major crisis involving powers in the Middle East and beyond.

ALL-OUT EFFORT

Intensive activity of SyAAF helicopters in support of garrisons isolated deep within areas controlled by insurgents, and attacks by L-39s and MiG-21s against insurgent-held areas in Aleppo and Idlib Provinces, resulted in the exposure of all these assets to increasing volumes of ground fire. Recognising the air force's impact on the battlefields, insurgents reacted with a series of attacks on SyAAF air bases. On 27 August, a Mi-8 was shot down by insurgent-operated ZU-23 flak over Qaboun district in Damascus. Another Mi-8 and a L-39 were shot down over Aleppo Province within the following 24 hours. Early on 28 August, Ahrar ash-Sham brigade raided the Afis AB (better known in the West as Taftanaz) for the first time, claiming the destruction and damage of 10 Mi-8s on the ground. Other insurgent groups put Abu ad-Duhor AB under siege, shot down two MiG-21s and damaged one Ilyushin Il-76 transport while this was landing there with supplies, between 30 August and 4 September. The Abdullah Ibn Salam Popular Defence Group overran the SA-5 SAM site outside Aftarees in Eastern Ghouta (in Rif Dimashq Province) on 27 August. Three days later the Mansour Battalion and Tawhid Brigade raided Kweres AB, east of Aleppo, destroying two L-39s and a Flamingo basic trainer, damaging two helicopters and causing up to 50 casualties to Air Defence Regiment 111. In all cases, the SyAAF reacted with vicious bombardments of these installations and nearby populated areas, forcing insurgents to withdraw, but eventually it was forced to cease operating helicopters over Damascus, Aleppo, Rastan and Talbiseh for the time being. L-39s from Ksheesh AB continued intensive operations over Aleppo, nevertheless, suffering four confirmed losses by the end of September.

The *de-facto* loss of air bases like Abu ad-Duhor, Afis and

No less than 11 Mi-8s and Mi-17s can be seen in this photograph of Afis AB taken before the base was raided by insurgents on 28 August 2012. A review of photographs and videos taken before that raid and documents captured after the fall of Afis AB in January 2013 have shown that No. 253 Squadron has lost Mi-8Ts serialled 1282, 1291, 1371 and 1387, and Mi-17s serialled 2921, 2922, 2924, 2926, 2931, 2936 and 2938 in August 2012. The sister-unit, No. 257 Squadron, lost the Mi-8Ts serialled 1277, 1283, 1374 and 1381, and Mi-17s serialled 2902, 2904 and 2911. (FSA release)

Two stills from different videos showing the SyAAF Mi-17 shot down over the Qaboun district of Damascus on 27 August 2012, and the insurgent Hebah al-Homsi who scored that kill using a ZU-23 flak installed on a technical. (FSA)

Kweres resulted in the SyAAF deploying Su-24s over Aleppo and Idlib, because targets in these areas were outside the range of most other fighter-bomber types. About a dozen of the available fighter-bombers of this type clocked up some 90 combat sorties over these two provinces alone by the end of 2012 – which was certainly a lot, considering that a much higher number of Su-22s flew only about 120 sorties.

In October 2012, the SMC managed to effect co-operation between the Idlib Military Council, various Islamist insurgent groups organised within the Syrian Islamist Front (SIF) and the JAN, and these deployed a combined force of about a dozen brigades to secure the town of Ma'rat an-Numaan. The capture of this crucial crossroad on the highway from Hama to Aleppo interrupted the main supply line for the government garrison in Aleppo. However, the first insurgent assault on the nearby Army base in Wadi ad-Dways failed and they were subsequently subjected to intensive air strikes. The situation in the Ma'arat an-Numaan area prompted the SyAAF to start launching between 180 and 200 combat sorties a day and, ultimately, this massive effort saved the Army base from being overrun. However, at least as often as they provided close support for besieged or nearly overrun ground units, SyAAF fighter-bomber pilots received strict orders to target bakeries and apartment areas in selected cities and towns, in order to cause civilian casualties. Two squadrons flying MiG-21s from Hama AB are known to have clocked up over 200 combat sorties against targets in this and the nearby Homs province by the end of the year. For example, on 18 October they killed at least 49 civilians (including 23 children) while targeting one bakery in Ma'arat an-Numaan. Similarly, they bombed the town of Haram after this was captured by insurgents, obliterating 30 apartment buildings and killing dozens.

By the end of October, the SyAAF suffered a confirmed cumulative loss of five L-39s, seven MiG-21s, one MiG-23BN, two Su-22s, and no less than 16 Mi-8 and Mi-17 helicopters, together with 22 pilots, other crew members and passengers KIA, 23 missing and five captured.[27] Only eight crew members – crews of two downed Mi-8 helicopters – were recovered. While most of the kills were scored with heavy machine guns and ZU-23 flaks 23mm calibre cannon, around a dozen fighter jets and helicopters was shot down by the relatively small number of SA-7 and SA-16 MANPADs captured by insurgents. The appearance of such weapons in the insurgent arsenal prompted the SyAAF to stop operating L-39s over Aleppo.

Despite losses, the air force further increased the pace of operations during November, flying up to 250 combat sorties a day by the middle of the month. It was during this period that the SyAAF began deploying Su-24s to hit targets in Aleppo and Idlib. At the same time, No. 819 Squadron SyAAF was repeatedly tasked to fly attacks on targets in north-eastern and eastern Syria, where the JAN spearheaded attacks that resulted in the capture of al-Thawra and Ba'ath hydroelectric dams in the Raqqa Province,

A Su-24MK loaded with eight bombs of unknown type over Jabal az-Zawiya, Idlib Province, in November 2012. (SNN)

Six Mi-8Ts and Mi-17s were left behind by the SyAAF at Marj as-Sultan AB on 24 November 2012, including Mi-8Ts serialled 1299 (seen in this photo), 1340 and 1387 (all partially dismantled), and Mi-17s serialled 2940 (damaged by small arms fire), 2944 (partially dismantled) and 2965. From what is known about their fate, all would have been destroyed during subsequent air strikes on this base.
(Army of Islam release)

the Teshreen Dam in Aleppo Province, and – on 22 November – a well-co-ordinated assault of the Mayadeen Artillery Base on the outskirts of Dayr az-Zawr. MiG-21s from Hama were mainly busy bombing Rastan and Qusayr, but these two towns subsequently became primary targets for units operating Su-22s and Su-24s, which flew about 160 combat sorties over the Homs Province by the end of 2012.

Except for launching local counterattacks in Aleppo, government ground forces largely remained idle during autumn 2012 – probably due to fuel shortages. It was only in Damascus that the RGD was very active, though the efforts of most of units of this division were concentrated on – literally – bulldozing entire neighbourhoods of southern Damascus. Led by Brig Gen Hussein Makhlouf, the operation in question resulted in the destruction and displacement of tens of thousands of civilians from Qaboun, Tadamoun, Almazza and Darayya, Harasta and Yalda, and summary executions of several hundred, between late August and late September. This operation was heavily supported by MiG-23s and Su-22s, which subsequently began targeting military bases in Eastern Ghouta overrun by insurgents, clocking up at least 500 sorties over this part of Syria by the end of the year. MiG-21s from Khelkhleh AB joined them in December, flying between 80 and 100 additional sorties.

Whether the SyAAF could have maintained such a pace of operations for much longer remains unknown, as does to what degree it depleted its available reserves of fuel (known to have been critical all around Syria at this time), spares and weapons. What is certain is that bad weather during December practically grounded much of the air force and the government therefore ordered the deployment of ballistic missiles against insurgent-held cities and towns instead. Over 300 such weapons –including Scud-B/Shahab-3s/Jowlan-2s, Zelzal/Misseloons and Fateh-110/Teshreens, but also a few FROG-7s – are known to have been fired against targets in northern Syria, largely in the Aleppo area, during 2013.

OFFENSIVE ON AIR BASES

Overall, with the exception of Aleppo and Wadi ad-Dwayf, most SyAAF efforts between August and December 2012 were in vain: the insurgents continued launching ever larger and better co-ordinated operations, bringing huge swathes of territory in northern, central and southern Syria under their control. For example, government forces are known to have lost 17 different bases and major checkpoints in Aleppo and Idlib Provinces between May 2012 and January 2013 alone, while the remaining few strongpoints were practically cut off from the outside world and entirely reliant for survival on supplies dropped from Mi-8 helicopters.

Starting in late November 2012, the insurgents launched a new offensive in Eastern Ghouta, capturing a number of local bases. On the 24th of that month, they overran the Marj as-Sultan AB, capturing five helicopters intact (although not operational) and destroying one on the ground. Around the same time, a map captured from an officer of the RGD had clearly shown that the government had lost control of almost the entire Eastern Ghouta.

During December 2012, the SMC reached agreements with the Liwa al-Tawhid (a major insurgent formation in the Aleppo area), SILF in Damascus, the Idlib Military Council (including the powerful Suqour ash-Sham Brigade) and the Farouq Brigade in Homs (which turned into a successful franchise that began arming and training insurgents in Rastan, Qusayr and even Dera'a) to launch additional joint operations. This resulted in several insurgent attacks on infrastructure of the government's centres of gravity and cleared specific positions instead of trying to gain territory in urban centres. For example, on 17 December, units of the Idlib and Homs Military Councils had overrun the town of Halfaya in Hama Province, capturing the weakly-defended yet excellently-stocked base of the 34th Armoured Brigade, together with between 12 and 15 intact T-72s and at least one ZSU-23-4. The government reacted by shelling Halfaya with artillery and then bombing it with Su-24s that killed up to 200 civilians, but subsequently the CO of the Hama-based No. 680 Squadron SyAAF, Col Amar, defected in protest over the atrocities.

Other such operations further degraded the SyAAF's capability to continue operating from air bases close to the frontlines. On 11 January 2013, the Taftanaz AB was finally overrun by a three-prong attack of insurgent factions from the SIF, SILF and JAN. This attack caught the government by surprise and resulted in the confirmed loss of nine additional Mi-8Ts, three Mi-17s and two Mi-25s, along with an already decommissioned Mi-8PS helicopter for electronic combat support. The commander of this base was killed during the assault, and insurgents captured 25 pilots, effectively destroying No. 253, No. 255 and No. 257 Squadrons. The SyAAF reacted with vicious air strikes by Su-22s that caused some damage to this base, but also demolished the nearby town. Although categorised as a 'success' by the government, this effort backfired: the surviving population of Taftanaz was largely forced to flee, but once their families were in the safety of refugee camps in Turkey, thousands of men returned to Syria to join the insurgency.

Only a week later, the insurgents in Rif Dimashq began launching attacks on more than 20 different government positions, including Damascus IAP. It was there that a Boeing 747 of Iran Air was damaged by ground fire while landing with

A JAN insurgent in front of an Mi-17 shot down while trying to escape from Afis AB on 11 January 2013. When Afis AB was overrun on 11 January, the SyAAF lost the Mi-8Ts serialled 1320 (badly damaged), 1344, 1353, 1355, 1394, 1395, 1397, and 1399 (badly damaged); Mi-17s serialled 2134, 2139, and 2936; and Mi-25s serialled 2802 and 2808. Most of these helicopters were destroyed during subsequent air strikes on this base, which began three days later. (ENN)

An Su-22M-4K pulling up after one of about 100 air strikes the SyAAF flew over Idlib Province in December 2012 and January 2013. Syria obtained only about 20 aircraft of this variant, some 14 of which remain in service with Sh'eirat-based No. 685 and T-4-based No. 827 Squadrons. Gauging by its camouflage colour (consisting of dark yellow sand and blue-green), this example appears to have been overhauled by "The Works" at Nayrab AB. (via R.S.)

The mass burial of dozens of civilians killed by SyAAF air strikes on Taftanaz in early April 2013. (via Y.A.)

a load of equipment for IRGC troops already present in Syria (see following chapter for details), on 13 January 2013. After overrunning a number of government positions – including the base of the 81st Air Defence Brigade (where some 200 troops defected to join them) – the insurgents withdrew in order not to expose themselves to the SyAAF, and then attacked again, among others entering the Yarmuk Palestinian Refugee Camp in southern Damascus. Controlled by organisations like the Popular Front for the Liberation of Palestine (PFLP), which sided with the government, and Hamas, which broke with Damascus (and Tehran) and withdrew its HQ to Qatar in 2012, the population of Yarmouk struggled to remain neutral. Those supporting the opposition eventually prevailed, but when insurgents entered, much of the population fled. The latter decision proved correct, as subsequently the government heavily bombarded the place and put it under siege, although it did not try an assault before February 2014.[28]

Through February 2013, the insurgents maintained pressure on the – meanwhile practically demolished, but still skilfully defended – Minakh, Nayrab and Kweres air bases, while concentrating on the capture of Ksheesh AB and the 'Base 80' south of Aleppo. A SyAAF Mi-8 helicopter was shot down over Kweres on 16 January while attempting to drop supplies, and a L-39 was shot down by MANPADs over Aleppo, two weeks later, killing its pilot. Following sustained insurgent attacks, Ksheesh AB was overrun on 1 February, by when the SyAAF had withdrawn most of its operational aircraft and all helicopters from there. Nevertheless, eight L-39ZOs were captured in – more or less – intact condition (together with nearly 50 derelict MiG-15UTIs and MiG-17Fs, all abandoned and used as decoys since the 1970s), one of which was destroyed during subsequent air attacks by Su-24s. Overall, February 2013 proved the worst month for the SyAAF so far. The air force suffered the confirmed loss of six Mi-8s (including two that attempted to resupply the besieged garrison at Minnakh AB), three MiG-21s and two Su-22s, while on 7 March No. 819 Squadron also lost a Su-24 shot down over Jabal az-Zawiya (the crew of two was captured).The same month was remarkable because insurgents overran ar-Raqqa City, thus becoming the first provincial capital to fall into their hands. A similar assault on Tabqah, some 60km west of Raqqa, was repulsed by government troops with support of the SyAAF, although the air force lost a MiG-21 and Su-22 during the fighting through the first half of April there (for cumulative SyAAF losses during the period June 2011 to July 2013, see Table 3). However, the capture of the 38th Air Defence Brigade's base outside Dera'a on 23 March, where insurgents secured sizeable stocks of SA-7 MANPADS; the appearance of Chinese-made FN-6 MANPADS in the Dayr az-Zawr area; and the capture of several SA-18 (or SA-24) MANPADS in Idlib Province during the spring of 2013 made the future of Bashar al-Assads's government appear rather gloomy.

The last insurgent success during this period of war occurred on 18 April 2013, when they overran the former Dhab'a AB outside al-Qusayr. Dhab'a was closed in 2009 but in recent years saw plenty of activity related to Iranian transports of arms and supplies to Hezbollah in Lebanon. This was quite a blow for Damascus, Tehran and for their proxies in Beirut, and a powerful reaction had to be expected.

A still from a video showing the retired Colonel of the UAE military, al-Abdouli, inside the cockpit of one of the L-39s captured at Ksheesh AB in February 2013. Abdouli was killed in fighting shortly later, but with some help from sources in Arab states along the Persian Gulf, and with spares found at this air base, the Islamic Front subsequently overhauled two L-39s. Only constant SyAAF attacks on Ksheesh have prevented these from flying combat operations. (via Tom Cooper)

Among many photographs found by insurgents when they captured the Ksheesh AB was this one showing a formation of L-39s during a training flight. Considering their camouflage pattern, all were overhauled by 'The Works' at Nayrab AB. Visible serial numbers are 2063 and 2121: the latter aircraft was shot down over Sheikh Najar in Aleppo Province on 15 October 2012. The crew of two ejected safely and was captured. (SyAAF)

A still from a video showing a scene that occurred in the Darayya district of Damascus on 24 January 2013. A RPG-29 round fired by insurgents (red circle) can be seen approaching a T-72 of the RGD: it hit the joint of the turret with the hull and penetrated the armour, causing a catastrophic internal combustion of ammunition. Only the commander – lucky enough to be thrown out of his hatch by the detonation – survived. Government forces lost at least 110 T-72s between June 2012 and June 2013. (Army of Islam release)

During the night from 17 to 18 April 2013, the Dhab'a AB outside Qusayr was overrun by insurgents. Out of service since 2009, Dhab'a's hardened aircraft shelters were housing only long-since abandoned aircraft, including MiG-21MFs with serial numbers 1523 and 1554, a MiG-21bis with serial number 2320 (seen on this photograph), two MiG-21UMs (including one with serial 2367) and one PZL Dromedar agricultural aircraft. (FSA release)

Table 4:
SyAAF losses for period June 2011–July 2013

Aircraft Type	Confirmed loss (shot down)	Confirmed loss (other reasons)	Remarks
Mi-8/17	46 (1 shot down by THK F-16)	26 (abandoned)	Practically all of abandoned helicopters destroyed in subsequent bombardments by SyAAF
Mi-25	2	2 (abandoned)	2 agandoned helicopters destroyed in subsequent bombardment by SyAAF
L-39	6	14	Most of captured aircraft destroyed in subsequent bombardment by SyAAF
MiG-21bis/UM	9	1 (defection to Jordan)	4 abandoned aircraft captured by insurgents
MiG-23BN	5		About 20 abandoned MiG-23MS/UBs captured or destroyed by insurgents
Su-22M-3K/M-4K	4		
Su-24MK	1		
Unknown fighter jet	5		Confirmation for the loss available in form of video but aircraft type unrecognisable
Transport aircraft	1		Yak-40 written off after hit by ground fire during landing at Dayr az-Zawr
Totals	30 fighter jets shot down 45 helicopters shot down 1 transport aircraft shot down	15 fighter jets abandoned or defected 28 helicopters abandoned	
Known personnel losses	376 pilots and crew members KIA; 36 pilots POW; 43 pilots and crew members MIA		

6
CONFLAGRATION

To many foreign observers it appeared that a collapse of the Syrian government was imminent during the spring of 2013, or at least only a matter of a few months away, but the war was to develop in an entirely unexpected fashion. Despite the creation of the SMC, the gradual dissolution of the Syrian insurgency continued through that spring, even more so once the extremist Islamist organisation The Islamic State of Iraq and the Levant (ISIL/ISIS) entered the country and began establishing itself in vast expanses of north-eastern Syria. The insistence of various foreign powers on providing aid directly to specific insurgent groups, and Western conditions of providing aid in exchange for political declarations and subjection to control by the SNC and SMC, resulted in quarrels and a rift within the FSA, and then in-fighting between various brigades and battalions. Amid increasing chaos and continous attacks by the government, many Syrians began requesting military aid from the West. However, because of poor intelligence about the situation in Syria, and public pressure at home, Western powers not only decided not to provide any, but also did a lot to suppress the support officially provided by the governments of Saudi Arabia and other Arab states. This made the aid provided via private channels in Qatar, Kuwait and elsewhere ever more important, in turn opening the doors for the most negative influences upon the Syrian public in general.

It was against this backdrop that the civil war in Syria was internationalised. Even this process developed in an unexpected fashion, with countries like Turkey and the USA strictly limited or restrained – respectively – from deploying military power against Assad's government, despite getting more than enough reasons to 'do something'. Simultaneously, the Iranian intervention on the side of the government was nearly overlooked – by the public inside and outside Syria, and even by foreign intelligence services.

TALKING SHOP
On 22 June 2012, a Turkish Air Force (Türk Havva Kuvvetleri, THK) RF-4ETM – serial 77-0314 – that flew narrowly outside Syrian airspace at a speed of 1,200km/h (745mph) and 2,255 metres (7,400ft) altitude was shot down by a SyAAF SA-3 SAM site positioned north of the port of Lattakia. The missile detonated near the left engine nozzle, throwing the jet out of control. It crashed into the Mediterranean Sea 13.84km (8.6 miles) from the Syrian coast, instantly killing the crew – including Capt Gökhan Ertan and Lt Hassan Hüseyin Aksoy.[29] While strongly protesting against this action, the Turkish government restrained from retaliation through military means, but continued providing aid to various Syrian insurgent groups, foremost the FSA. Indeed, it took a series of Syrian government artillery attacks on Turkish border villages and about a dozen of Turkish civilian casualties for the government in Ankara to order the 3rd Artillery Regiment of its Army to return fire on 22 October 2012.[30]

Contrary to the Iranian decision to support the government of Bashar al-Assad by most available means, Turkey restrained from retaliation and limited its activity to providing safe haven to selected insurgent groups. Similarly, although the Syrian government continued crossing the 'red line' announced by US President Barak

Obama, by continuous deployment of chemical weapons against insurgent-held areas, Washington limited its reaction to reaching an agreement with Moscow, whereby Damascus officially declared and then promised to destroy its stockpiles of such armament. Repeated delays and postponements in the schedule prompted no reaction from the USA or the West in general. While some European powers – foremost France – understood the seriousness of the situation and realities in Syria, and exercised plenty of pressure for an intervention, their efforts were fruitless. With the US public – war-weary after nearly 10 years of fruitless wars in Iraq and Afghanistan – happily ignoring rich traditions of Syrian government involvement in international terrorism and the Iranian military intervention, and convincing itself that the civil war in Syria is a conflict between a 'secular government and al-Qaida', the Obama administration swiftly concluded that is of no pressing interest for the USA. Practically all European NATO members followed in the same fashion, and thus Western involvement in this conflict remained limited to deliveries of relief aid for Syrian refugees in Jordan and Turkey, and on-off deliveries of support equipment to the FSA, most of which had next to no effect on developments on the battlefield. On the contrary, the West – and especially the Obama administration – repeatedly exercised strong pressure upon the Saudi government to limit its support for the insurgency. Understanding what is at stake in Syria, considering not only al-Qaida but also Iran its arch enemies, and already in a clinch with Qatar over its support for the Syrian Moslem Brotherhood, the Saudi government attempted to act on its own. However, Saudi attempts at supporting selected groups at their own discretion were practically overruled by the US government. In summary, all of these developments not only frustrated many Syrian insurgents but furthered the already significant rifts between different insurgent groups, exposing them to influence from Islamist extremists to a degree beforehand unknown in Syria.

AL-QUDS TO THE RESCUE
Although the Shi'a Islamist Iran and the 'secular' government of Syria are not 'natural' allies, the Islamic Republic of Iran (IRI) government has been maintaining close ties with Damascus since the early 1980s, and has developed a core interest to continue maintaining a strong position in the country. This is partly related to its need for Syria as an Arab ally against the Sunni Arab states – foremost Saudi Arabia – but especially for Syrian support for the Iranian proxy in Lebanon, the Hezbollah. Following the motto 'we're not like the Americans, we don't abandon our friends', the government in Tehran was very swift to start providing aid to the government in Damascus.

As usual in such cases, the methods in which the Islamic Revolutionary Guard Corps (IRGC) became involved more resembled a combined – intelligence and commercial – enterprise than a classic, conventional military intervention. Initially, the IRGC made use of several dozen experienced officers assigned to its Failaq al-Quds that were present in Syria with the primary task of overseeing the transfer of arms and supplies to Hezbollah in Lebanon. Reinforced by several hundred IRGC volunteers, these were deployed to advise – and sometimes openly support – government forces in nearly all of their early operations against mass protests. Otherwise, the IRGC limited its activity to provision of 'courier services' for the money Tehran began providing to save

Major General Qassem Suleimani, commander of the Quds Force of the IRGC. This pragmatic, non-religious but staunchly nationalist Iranian had earned himself a reputation as a courageous warrior during the war with Iraq in the 1980s, and that of a notorious 'grey eminence' while running the Shi'a insurgency against the US-led occupation of Iraq in the 2000s. (via Mark Lepko)

Two combatants of the Liwa Abu Fadl al-Abbas, one of the first Iraqi Shi'a militias recruited by the IRGC and deployed in Syria. Although receiving on average only two weeks of training in Iran, many members of such units used to serve with the Iraqi Army and Police trained by US forces in the 2000s, and are in possession of significant combat experience. (LAFA release)

the Assads from bankruptcy, and advice in combat operations. Despite the presence of such high-ranking IRGC officers as Brig Gen Hassan Shateri (former CO Failaq al-Quds in Lebanon), their overall influence on the battlefields of the Syrian Civil War remained limited for the first two years of war.

The situation underwent the first major change after the fall of Dha'ba. During the following weeks, the commander of the Quds Force, Maj Gen Qassem Suleimani, arrived in Syria again. In command of the Quds Force since 1998, Suleimani is practically the 'executioner' of orders he receives from Vahid Hagganian, who in turn is the link between the 'Supreme Leader of the Islamic Revolution' (the *de-facto* strongman of Iran), Ali Khamenei, and top IRGC commanders. More recently, he was the key person in organising the IRGC-controlled Shi'a resistance against the US-led occupation of Iraq, the Badr Brigade (the armed wing of the Shi'a party named the Supreme Council for the Islamic Revolution in Iraq) and instrumental in establishing the government of the Islamic Dawa Party and Prime Minister Nouri Kamil Mohammed Hassan al-Maliki in power in Baghdad.

Within just a few days of inspecting the situation, Suleimani concluded the Syrian military was 'useless'. This resulted in two ideas: organising a Syrian equivalent of the 'Basiji' Corps (a popular militia run by the IRGC since the time of the war with Iraq) or a complete reorganisation and re-training of remaining Syrian military and intelligence assets. For this purpose, Suleimani

brought in Brig Gen Hossein Hamedani (former CO Basiji Corps), who subsequently became instrumental in the establishment of the NDF, and Brig Gen Jamali (former CO Kerman Security Council, with extensive experience in fighting against Afghan and Pakistani drug dealers and asymmetric warfare), who received the responsibility of reorganising the government's intelligence services. It was under these circumstances that IRGC officers became deeply involved in training various pro-government militias, and then in setting up an elaborate system to monitor insurgent communications.

However, because the Iranians needed time to re-train the Syrian military while the Syrian government's position was meanwhile precarious, Suleimani had to buy time. So he requested Shi'a militias in Iraq to establish units that could be deployed inside Syria almost immediately. Simultaneously, he prompted Hassan Nasrallah, Hezbollah's leader, to also deploy his fighters into Syria and – understanding that his organisation would find it hard to survive without Dhab'a – Nasrallah reacted as requested. Combined together, all these deployments, reorganisations and measures were to turn the tide of the war.

BATTLE OF AL-QUSAYR

The primary aim of Hezbollah units that began deploying into Syria during March 2013 became the town of al-Qusayr, a major insurgent stronghold in south-western Homs province, overlooking a significant stretch of the border with Lebanon. With two small Hezbollah brigades on hand – supported by three task forces from the 4th AD (the latter including detachments from the former 3rd, 7th and 10th Divisions) – Suleimani planned the offensive to be completed within five days: government units were to surround and block the area, after which the Hezbollah would move in and mop up. To the surprise of the Iranians and Hezbollah, however, not all the involved Syrian units welcomed them. Not only were some of the local commanders selling intelligence, equipment and ammunition to the insurgents, but a few openly co-operated with them. On the first day of the offensive, 4 April 2013 – whether by mistake or design – SyAAF fighter bombers even hit Hezbollah positions instead of those held by insurgents.

Nominally operating under the auspices of the FSA, the 17 different insurgent groups holding the area put up stiff resistance, and launched several counterattacks. Because government troops repeatedly refused to follow Hezbollah into battle and withdrew, the Lebanese Shi'a were several times outflanked and suffered unexpectedly heavy casualties. Their first assault attempt on al-Qusayr was beaten back, on 19 May.[31] However, cut off from outside support, the insurgents could not hold out forever. Concerned about the fate of over 25,000 civilians and more than 1,000 injured fighters, their leaders decided to try to evacuate by reaching either the border to Lebanon or insurgent-held areas north and east of al-Qusayr. The operation was launched during the evening of 4 June and resulted in a partial disaster, with hundreds of insurgents and civilians killed while punching out of the siege and marching in open terrain under heavy artillery fire. The Hezbollah secured al-Qusayr a day later in the course of a nocturnal attack that met only little resistance.

Meanwhile, al-Quds officers began sorting out the situation in Damascus, where insurgents had not only cut off the highway to the IAP, but also the districts of Kfar Sousa, Barzeh, Jobar and Zamalka, during February. In cooperation with the RGD, the Iraqi Shi'a militias deployed with the help of Boeing 747s of the Islamic Republic of Iran Air Force (IRIAF), IranAir and Ilyushin Il-76 transports of the IRGC Air & Space Force (IRGCASF) from Mashhad in Iran to the IAP, having first taken care to secure the highway and the Sayida Zainab before launching attacks on Moadamiyeh, Yarmouk and al-Husseniya in the south. This offensive caught the disunited insurgents by surprise, and was followed by a major advance of the IRGC, Iraqis, the RGD and 4th AD on Harran al-Awamid, Qaysa and Jarba, east and north of Damascus IAP. By the end of March, they had not only reopened the highway connecting the Syrian capital with the airport, but also put three large insurgent-held pockets in Rif Dimashq under siege. With this, however, the government forces ran out of steam again. Not only were their operations greatly hampered by the lack of troop strength and fuel, but some Iraqi Shi'a units began fighting each other for control of Sayida Zainab, while others refused to take orders from both the IRGC and the Syrians. Finally, al-Quds officers in command of this hoge-poge of assets were not keen to risk high losses while assaulting the insurgent-held southern suburbs of Damascus: with a number of ex-SyAA units undergoing training with the help of Iranian and Hezbollah advisers, and in the process of being reorganised as the NDF, conservation of remaining assets remained a priority for the time being.

Defence of the 'Shrine of Sayida Zainab' – a religious site in the southern district of Damascus that saw plenty of Iranian pilgrimage in the 2000s – against attacks by al-Qaida is the official reason for the deployment of Iraqi Shi'a militias in Syria. This rare photograph of that shrine was posted on the internet by a LAFA member. (LAFA release)

A fighter of the Liwa Abu Fadl al-Abbas seen with an RGD T-72AV. Since the spring of 2013, several militias recruited by the IRGC in Iraq, Azerbaijan and elsewhere have been deployed as 'mechanised infantry' of the Republican Guards Division. (LAFA release)

A ZSU-23-4 Shilka SPAAG in the Qusayr area in May 2013. With no threat of air attacks, they are usually deployed in ground combat mode, in which their high rate of fire proved highly effective in fighting against insurgent ATGM teams. (via M.P.)

Quds Force officers working with the Syrian military were surprised to find out that many of their Syrian counterparts were co-operating with insurgents. Indeed, in August 2013 the Liwa al-Islam released a video from which these two stills were taken, showing a column of uparmoured T-72AVs and BMP-1s it said it bought from an officer of the 4th AD. (LI release)

Fighters of one of the pro-government militia with a BMP-1 IFV during the Battle of Qusayr in May 2013. (via M.P.)

THE SECOND MOST IMPORTANT MAN IN SYRIA

Under such circumstances it was early July 2013 before Suleimani agreed to launch an operation to improve government positions in Homs, nearly two-thirds of which were meanwhile held by insurgents. During March 2013, an insurgent break-out attempt combined with attacks on government positions from the direction of Rastan and Talbiseh had managed to loosen the months-long siege of the city and bring some supplies to the Bab Amr and Khalidya districts. Only a vicious campaign of SyAAF attacks prevented a collapse of government positions in several parts of the city. Following a week of heavy artillery and aerial bombardment, IRGC-led and supported government troops assaulted the Old City and Khaldiyeh districts, in early July. Advancing slowly and methodically, they had captured most of both before this operation had to be stopped.

On 4 August, ten insurgent brigades launched an offensive into north-eastern Lattakia Province. Despite rugged terrain, they swiftly captured 12 villages, put the Qardaha – the home town of the Assad family – under artillery fire and threatened to advance on Lattakia. After some hesitation – apparently caused by a dispute between Suleimani and his staff, and the government in Damascus over whether to continue the offensive into Homs or react to the insurgent offensive – the Death Brigade NDF (elements of the former 1st Division, primarily consisting of the former 76th Brigade) was rushed north along the coastal highway. The unit was reinforced by at least two NDF battalions while under way, and received vivid support from the SyAAF before launching its counterattack. This succeeded in forcing the insurgents back and recovering most of the lost villages, though not without heavy losses for the government.

On 6 August, the garrison of the Minakh AB collapsed after 10 months of siege, some escaping to nearly Kurdish and Shi'a enclaves while the rest was overrun in the final insurgent assault. Fifteen days later, various insurgent groups, in co-operation with the JAN, had overrun the garrison of Khanasir, in southern Aleppo Province, decimating a battalion of IRGC troops in the process. In this fashion, the insurgents had cut off the government's last supply route into Aleppo City. The situation was soon to experience further escalation, as the insurgents then began to invest the town of as-Safira, about 100km south of Aleppo and the site of one of the biggest production and storage facilities for chemical weapons in Syria. Almost simultaneously, insurgents inside Aleppo – reinforced by several shipments of ATGMs and ammunition from Saudi Arabia, and improved co-operation between different units – had stopped a local government offensive and then launched a powerful counterattack that resulted in them recapturing Sallhaddin and Hamadaniya districts before continuing into New Aleppo. Under pressure, the government

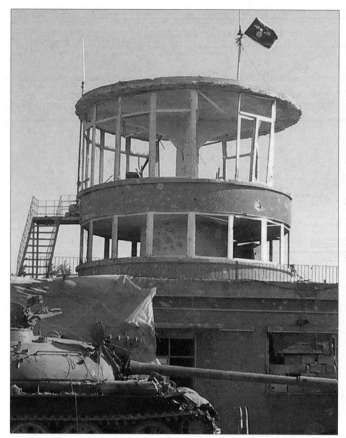

This T-55AMV operated by the NDF was knocked out during the last insurgent advance in Aleppo in August 2013. (via Y.A.)

The old control tower of Minakh AB (constructed during the time of the French Mandate) on the morning of 6 August 2013, when this base was overrun by insurgents. Because the final assault was preceded by the attack of an ISIS suicide bomber, extremist Islamists rushed to claim this as a victory for themselves: the base was to remain under their control until early 2014. The SyAAF is known to have lost at least five Mi-8s at Minakh. (ISIS release)

Members of an unknown Iraqi Shi'a militia on the streets of Aleppo. At least two units of these combatants were rushed to reinforce the government garrison in Aleppo during the summer of 2013. (LAFA release)

replaced garrison commander Lt Gen Mohammed Khadour with Lt Gen Essam Zahreddine (former CO 104th Brigade RGD) and requested Iranians to lift the siege of the city; the supply situation was already dire and with the coming winter could not have been expected to improve.

The loss of Khanasir was something of a turning point in Iranian involvement in the war. Until that time the IRGC's al-Quds operatives were primarily providing advisory and material support. They were instrumental in the reorganisation of what was left of the Syrian military and the deployment of the Hezbollah and Iraqi Shi'a militias inside Syria. They commanded the latter two forces during battles for Qusayr and in Homs, but rarely became directly involved in combat operations. Subsequently, Suleimani and his aides were to leave no doubt about who was in command of the entire Syrian military. All of their counterparts fighting for the government – from the Syrian Minister of Defence down to every company commander – were instructed that Suleimani was 'the second most important man in Syria' and to strictly listen to and follow every single one of his orders, without any disputes or discussions.

In the course of negotiations with Tehran, Suleimani requested – and was granted – additional IRGC troops and materiel necessary to reopen the supply route to Aleppo during late August. This resulted in a sharp increase in Iranian supply flights into Damascus IAP during the late summer of 2013, with several transport aircraft landing there every day. Apart from carrying large amounts of arms, ammunition and fuel, the aircraft brought in a sizeable IRGC

battlefield command staff and the personnel of an entire brigade of the 8th 'Najaf' Armoured Division IRGC. Due to Tehran's continued insistence on 'minimal footprint' of their presence, the Pasdaran (IRGC) brought very little of their own equipment with them: instead, they were equipped with T-72s, BMP-2s, tube artillery, Multiple Launch Rocket Systems (MLRS) and other armament of the RGD (which was meanwhile running short on troops because of heavy losses from earlier fighting).

The next to arrive was a battalion-sized special forces contingent known as Seraya Tli-e-Khorasani, followed by additional contingents of Iraqi Shi'a, and then a sizeable team of IRGCASF officers, pilots and ground personnel. Despite their total numbers, the IRGC forces in Syria are extremely hard to track down: the units in question are not massive nor spread over the battlefield like Roman legions, or operating independently from other government forces. Instead, they are tightly integrated with Hezbollah and Iraqi Shi'a militias, and the RGD, or deployed in small detachments that command the NDF and BPM units, and other pro-government militias, like that of the Syrian Socialist National Party (SSNP).

Following several weeks of intensive training, Suleimani's new force was deployed for a test-attack on the Yalda district of southern Damascus, next to Sayida Zainab. In late September, a surprise nocturnal assault – something unheard of in the Syrian Civil War until that time – practically overran the local insurgents. Despite minimal support of artillery, armour and air power, the Iranians and Iraqis secured the entire area within only 48 hours.

Lt Gen Mohammed Khadour (foreground, right), CO of government troops in Aleppo until July 2013, addressing his combatants before he was replaced by Lt Gen Essam Zahreddine. (SANA)

A 'home-made' mortar operated by insurgents in Aleppo. Different variants of such weapons, most of them using butane bottles as ammunition, have been constructed by insurgents in a number of Syrian cities. Some are capable of collapsing a multi-storey building with a single shot. (FSA release)

Lt Gen Essam Zahreddine, former CO of the 104th Brigade RGD, was put in command of the Aleppo garrison during the crisis that developed in late summer 2013. He earned himself a fearful reputation among insurgents and has survived numerous assassination attempts. (Zahreddine collection)

NORTHERN STORM

By early October 2013, Suleimani re-deployed part of his troops from Damascus via Tadmor into the eastern Hama Province, where they joined task forces of the 4th AD (*de-facto* now all operated by the NDF). In this fashion he created a combination that was to become characteristic of this conflict: small, crack IRGC (or Hezbollah) units, supported by heavy weaponry of the RGD, 4th AD and SyAAF, followed by NDF units deployed to secure recaptured positions.[32] Although rumours about the pending 'government offensive' in the direction of Aleppo – 'Operation Northern Storm' – were prematurely released to the public, the insurgents ignored them and remained busy investing as-Safira. Therefore the assault on Khanasir took them by surprise and was over almost as soon as it began: during the evening of 2 October, IRGC special troops were deployed by helicopters behind insurgent positions. The chaos their appearance caused was exploited by Iraqi Shi'a infantry to infiltrate and then assault the town. Khanasir was safely in government hands by the morning of 4 October and an IRGC supply unit – deployed instead of a Syrian military logistical system, which often spoiled the results of earlier successes – rushed 20 convoys of trucks loaded

with fuel, ammunition, food and reinforcements to the beleaguered garrison in Aleppo.

The assault on insurgent positions in the north-eastern part of as-Safira began on 15 October and saw some of the most bitter fighting in the war to that date, as the insurgents – often supported by captured armour and artillery pieces – offered bitter resistance. It took a massive dose of artillery and air strikes to force them to withdraw on 31 October. The SyAAF MiG-23MFs and MiG-29s were particularly active during this operation, firing plenty of S-24 unguided rockets of 240mm calibre (and their laser-homing variants, S-25), and Kh-23 and Kh-29 guided missiles. The reason for the deployment of these interceptor types for ground-attack purposes might appear doubtful, but it should be borne in mind that after more than a year of intensive operations, much of the actual SyAAF fighter-bomber fleet was worn out and in need of overhaul. Also, al-Quds officers were seeking to improve the air force's combat effectiveness, resulting in the deployment of more modern – and lethal – weapons, deployed from aircraft equipped with better fire-control systems.

By 3 November, the Iranians and Iraqis advanced on al-Bab, which was taken in another nocturnal attack, before their advance was stopped by insurgents who had recently taken Base 80 (former barracks of the 80th Brigade) together with extensive stocks of ammunition. Suleimani had spent several days rotating his units before deploying two NDF task forces, reinforced by Iraqis, to push towards Nayrab AB on 10 November. Finding no other way around this stronghold, the IRGC launched another nocturnal heliborne insertion of special forces, but this failed because the helicopters landed inside an unknown minefield north of Base 80, where at least two were destroyed and up to 24 crew members and special forces operatives killed or captured (all survivors were summarily executed by insurgents).[33] The fighting for Base 80 was heavy, as were losses on both sides: the Iraqis even lost one of their brigade commanders. Nevertheless, the insurgent front lines south of Aleppo collapsed under relentless pressure: amid consistent factionalising and outright infighting between different groups, and due to increasing pressure by ISIS, most native rebels withdrew into central and eastern Aleppo, leaving only the JAN to provide resistance in the area between that city and the Kweres AB, 40km east of it.

SyAAF MiG-29s armed with B-8M rocket pods over Damascus in October 2013. Once much of the air force's MiG-23BN and Su-22 fleets were worn out due to intensive operations, MiG-29s were pressed into service as fighter-bombers. Since October 2013, they are primarily deployed in support of major, IRGC-led operations, foremost deploying B-8M pods for unguided rockets and PGMs – including, apparently, Iranian-made laser-homing bombs of 250kg calibre, for which target designation is provided by UAVs. (via R.S.)

Two SyAAF MiG-29s following an overhaul and upgrade to MiG-29SMT-like standard by 'The Works' at Nayrab IAP in 2012. They did not receive additional fuel cells in the spin behind the cockpit, but now had a weapons system enabling them to deploy R-77 (AA-12 Adder) medium-range air-to-air missiles, and a wide range of PGMs. (Photo by R.S.)

An SyAAF MiG-23MF interceptor armed with B-8M pods, about to attack a target in Eastern Ghouta in November 2013. The same variant was used in conjunction with – obsolete but reliable – Kh-23 (AS-7 Kedge) guided missiles to strike a number of important targets in the Aleppo and Idlib Provinces, around the same time, including HQs of major insurgent units, often causing heavy losses. (Photo by LensDimashqi)

A SyAAF MiG-23MF interceptor armed with Kh-23 (AS-7 Kerry) guided missiles over East Ghouta, in November 2013. MiG-23MFs armed this way flew several highly successful strikes against insurgent HQs in Aleppo and Idlib Provinces, around the same time. (Photo by LensDimashqi)

Several types of Iranian-made UAVs are in service with government forces, but foremost with Quds Force/IRGC and Hezbollah units deployed in Syria. This Mohajeer-4 UAV (also known as 'Pahpad') was photographed over southern Damascus in July 2013. (via R.S.)

ISIS operated relatively few heavy weapons in northern Syria, including a handful of T-55s and heavy technicals confiscated from different insurgent groups. This truck carrying the (Soviet-made) 57mm calibre S-60 flak was photographed by a British Jihadist who fought for the extremists in late 2013. Heavier equipment was actually not necessary because ISIS's primary targets became lightly-protected insurgent-controlled towns and villages, well away from the front lines, which they found easy to secure by surprise. (Photo by Abu Layth Briton/ISIS)

The scene of a strike by one of dozens of ballistic missiles that hit insurgent-held parts of Aleppo on 19 February 2013. (Aleppo Media Centre)

According to sources within NATO forces deployed to bolster the defences of Turkey, Syrian government forces have fired at least 300 intermediate-range ballistic missiles against insurgent-held areas in northern Syria alone during the first half of 2013. This is an Iranian-made Zelzal missile – named Miseloon in Syria – that can carry a 600kg warhead over a range of about 200km.
(Syrian Ministry of Defence)

ENDGAME IN DAMASCUS

During the summer and autumn of 2013, the situation of insurgents in different pockets they held in southern Damascus and the surrounding area began to worsen. They were exposed to several attacks with chemical weapons –the biggest of which, launched on 21 August, caused the deaths of hundreds of civilians and an outburst of protests on the international diplomatic scene – and then subjected to a siege by reinforced government forces, which made it impossible for insurgents to resupply. During mid-October, this prompted significant parts of local SIF, SILF and Army of Islam groups to withdraw from Eastern Ghouta in the direction of the Qalamoun Range. Suleimani reacted by deploying one brigade of Hezbollah – reinforced by elements of the former 18th Division and the 155th Missile Brigade (both meanwhile reorganised and re-trained as parts of the NDF) – in a pursuit. However, this operation – strongly supported by the SyAAF – was spoiled by insurgent attacks on large military storage facilities in Mahin and Sadad, which contained extensive stocks of ammunition and a number of stored tanks and artillery pieces. Furthermore, another insurgent group attacked Damascus IAP during the night of 28 to 29 October. Re-directing his forces, Suleimani forced the insurgents to withdraw back into the Qalamoun mountains in the north, and back into their pockets in southern Damascus, by 30 October. However, the opportunity to knock out a large concentration of enemies with a single blow passed, and they were to continue causing problems.

Limited by another shortage of fuel (most of which was used for Northern Storm), Suleimani subsequently limited the operation of his forces in the Damascus area to tightening the grip around besieged insurgent-held areas. However, he did not miss a chance to further improve the training of these forces. For example, the al-Quds officers began to train Iraqi and Syrian tank drivers in deploying counter-ATGM measures – mainly through evasion tactics, but also in conjunction with ground observers who were warning them about missiles and calling artillery strikes in response. Furthermore, his officers began insisting on air support by MiG-29s equipped with B-8 pods for unguided rockets: these proved not only capable of reacting to calls for support at shorter notice than other fighter-bombers in service with the SyAAF, but also of delivering its ordnance in more precise fashion, while 80mm calibre rockets proved more effective than the older S-5s fired from UV-16-57 and UV-32-57 pods.

On the back of the combined Iranian-Iraqi force that re-opened the supply corridor to Aleppo, several pro-government militias followed to secure reconquered areas. This photograph shows members of one of the SSNP-battalions in southern Aleppo in late 2013. All of their arms, uniforms and equipment are from former Army stocks, and they are practically indistinguishable from other native pro-government forces. (SSNP release)

New tactics and armament began to have effect by mid-December 2013. Like artillery units of the SyAA before, the insurgent artillery proved inflexible, unable to rapidly switch between different targets. Many pieces were knocked out by air strikes, while others fell into disrepair because of poor maintenance and lack of spares. Never particularly well supplied with ATGMs and MANPADs, the insurgents in and around Damascus were soon left with a few B-10 recoilless guns as their only heavy weapon, and there was a chronic shortage of ammunition for these. For all practical purposes, they were finished, left only with assault rifles and machine guns for their defence. Even so, they were not ready to give up. On 11 December, the insurgents launched an offensive into Eastern Ghouta, attempting a breach in the direction of the Qalamoun Range. Following a spate of early successes, their advances became bogged down when reaching a number of military bases constructed well before the war in a circle about 30km outside Damascus, or well-protected towns like Adra in the north and Qaysa in the south. Most of the insurgents in isolated pockets in southern Damascus and central Homs were forced to enter ceasefire negotiations with the government, or face a near certain death due to starvation, lack of water and diseases, by the end of the year.

A NDF-operated T-62 MBT at the entrance to the town of Nabk, briefly occupied by the JAN in late November 2013. Making good use of flat and open terrain, the IRGC-led National Defence Force skilfully deployed its heavy weapons to cause heavy losses to the insurgents. (NDF release)

Except for a few videos released accidentally (usually due to a mistake by the Syrian Military Censorship), visual evidence of the IRGC presence in Syria is extremely rare. Nevertheless, families of 'martyrs fallen in the defence of Sayida Zainab Shrine' occasionally commemorate the death of their sons on the internet, like in the case of IRGC combatant Mehdi Azizi, killed in Syria on 2 August 2013. (Iranian internet)

A Hezbollah fighter with a Burkan (or Failaq-2) multiple rocket launcher in Syria in late 2013. (Hezbollah release)

CONCLUSIONS

Concurrent with factionalisation and infighting between insurgent groups, and the appearance of extremist Islamists that destroyed most activist and insurgent networks in north-eastern and northern Syria, the Iranian military intervention was a major new factor on the battlefields of the Syrian Civil War in 2013. It came as a strategic surprise for Syrian insurgents and their supporters abroad who, expecting an imminent fall of Assad's government, gravely underestimated the resolve – and capabilities – of the IRGC and that of the Hezbollah. As in Lebanon and Iraq before, Tehran had once again proven ready to take the costs – monetary, materiel and in terms of human resources – necessary to achieve its aims, resulting in a military operation that became much more than just 'helping a friend in need'. Not obvious at first, and due to the passivity and indecisiveness of the West and its Arab allies like Saudi Arabia, as well as the malicious intentions of Qatar and Turkey, the Iranian intervention in Syria was only gaining momentum during late 2013: through early 2014 it began to directly threaten the very existence of the Syrian insurgency.

Under present circumstances, it is hard to predict in what direction this war might develop. The appearance of ISIS created lots of chaos and confusion between insurgents in northern Syria in 2012 and 2013. However, a relatively short – yet well-organised and executed – counteroffensive by only one part of insurgent forces, launched in January 2014, forced ISIS to withdraw from Aleppo and Idlib Provinces and its future even in such distant parts of Syria as Dayr az-Zawr Province are presently anything but certain. Iranian involvement was further intensified in February and March 2014, when the Quds Force supervised a major Hezbollah offensive that dispersed a large insurgent concentration in the Qalamoun Range, forcing many of them to flee over the border to Lebanon. It can be expected that similar operations are to follow in Eastern Ghouta, the fall of which would certainly deliver a severe blow for the entire insurgent movement. On the other side, several new – Saudi-supported – alliances of moderate insurgents made an appearance, establishing themselves in control of most of the Dera'a and Aleppo Provinces. Although their operations are repeatedly constrained by US-imposed limitations on the type of arms and equipment the Saudis are permitted to provide, they have shown much improved skills in command and control, as well as in execution of their operations, and a better discipline than ever before.

Obviously, although most Syrians are still fighting on behalf of the government or the insurgency, the war in Syria is not going to be decided by them, but by foreign powers fighting for their own interests.

Appendix I
CATALOGUE OF ARMED GROUPS FIGHTING IN SYRIA, 2011-2013

The Syrian Civil War is meanwhile a conflict involving as many as 50 different organisations, which in turn are running up to around 1,500 different military or para-military groups and units varying in size from companies to battalions and brigades. Pro-government forces are dominated by militias run on behalf of Iran or different Syrian political parties and movements, reinforced by para-military groups from about half-a-dozen other Arab states. Genuine – and native – insurgent forces are grouped within several major umbrella organisations, each of which became a de-facto proxy of anther foreign power. Various Syrian ethnic groups – primarily Kurds, but lately Assyrians too – have established their own para-military forces for self-defence purposes. Finally, while attracting plenty of media attention and causing much trouble for native insurgents, a relatively small group of foreign Jihadists is fighting its own war in Syria too. This chapter provides a general overview of major military and para-military forces active as of early 2014.

Government Forces: From Army to Militia
Of the three branches of the Syrian military existent in 2011, only one – the Syrian Arab Air Force – remains operational as of early 2014. Like all other major units, the Republican Guards Division has suffered extensive losses and remains operational only due to an infusion of IRGC units and Iraqi Shi'a militias within its ranks. All other major Army units – including the 4th Armoured Division and majority of Special Forces Command – were reorganised as elements of the NDF. Their remnants are operational in the form of small task forces, consisting of an original Army cadre reinforced by companies and battalions from various para-military groups. The small Syrian Arab Navy – much of which was in poor condition already in the 2000s – saw a short deployment in support of a general clampdown on protests in the Lattakia area in autumn 2011. The majority of its ships (and all submarines) are meanwhile non-operational, and even patrolling activity along Syrian maritime borders is limited to an absolute minimum.

Quds Corps/Force (the Army of the Guardians of the Islamic Revolution, IRGC)
As described above, the command cadre of the IRGC's Failaq al-Quds deployed in Syria is meanwhile in control of practically all of the government's military operations. The IRGC is not part of the conventional Iranian military, but an ideologically-driven militia, including ground, aerospace, naval, missile, information warfare and intelligence forces, and the para-military Basiji militia, the primary purpose of which is protection of that country's clerical and political system. Two brigade-sized IRGC formations are deployed in Syria. One brigade from the 8th 'Najaf' Armoured Division IRGC is active under the guise of the RGD, primarily in Damascus and surrounding areas. The other brigade includes a battalion of special forces named Seraya Tli-e-Khorasani, members of which are close to hard-line circles around the former Iranian president Mahmoud Ahmadinejad. More importantly, officers of the **Failaq al-Quds** (Jerusalem Corps) of the IRGC – which is a special operations unit handling activities abroad – are meanwhile supervising the activities of practically the entire Syrian military and all allied forces.

National Defence Force (NDF)
The Quwwat ad-Difa al-Watani (Arabic for the NDF) came into being from a combination of hundreds of already existing Popular Committees, the Shabiha and civilian volunteers, with remnants of various SyAA units, either mauled due to combat losses or weakened by defections. Equipped with armament from SyAA stocks, maintained with Iranian financing and trained by the IRGC and Hezbollah, it grew to around 60,000 personnel by mid-2013. Although originally consisting of units deployed in their local areas, the NDF has meanwhile practically replaced the Army: a significant part of it was organised into battalions that are assigned to command cadre of former SyAA units, where they act as infantry. Among dozens of examples of such 'newly-created' units now run under the NDF-flag are the former 76th Armoured Brigade (1st AD) in Idlib; the 85th Brigade (11th AD) in Hama and the former 17th Division deployed in the Rastan area. Other ex-Army and now NDF units are operational in Rif Dimashq, Dera'a and Homs.

Meanwhile there is no outside distinction between NDF and former Army units – with one, but important, exception: the IRGC and Hezbollah prefer to work with newly-created NDF and BPM units, instead of those originating from the former Army, because they found their troops better led, motivated, disciplined and therefore more effective in combat. Correspondingly, the NDF and BPM are nowadays one of the most important native military forces fighting for the government of Bashar al-Assad. Even should the Iranians suddenly stop their involvement (something that presently appears extremely unlikely), their involvement in creating and commanding these forces has made it sure that even in the case of Assad's fall, their remnants would still be well-suited to transform themselves into a capable insurgent network.

Iraqi Shi'a Militias
Under the auspices of the Iranian Quds Corps, a significant number of Iraqi Shi'a militias have been recruited through The Movement for the Party of God the Outstanding (Harakat Hezbollah al-Nujaba), and deployed to Syria, supposedly to 'protect the Shrine of Saida Zaynab' (situated in the southern suburbs of Damascus). This network is primarily drafting combatants for units like Asa'ib al-Haq, Kata'ib Hezbollah, Liwa Ammar Ibn Yasir, Liwa al-Imam al-Hassan al-Mujtaba, and – since November 2013 – for Liwa al-Ahmad. The recruited Iraqi Shi'a are usually given a minimum of two weeks of military training on one of the IRGC bases in Iran (often in Mashhad), before travelling to Damascus by plane (less often by bus). Nearly all the units in question are commanded by an IRGC officer cadre and as such integrated within the IRGC chain of command in Syria, which results in them usually co-operating well with the NDF and BPM, but less so with other armed groups fighting for the government. Because of their relatively good training, discipline and high combat effectiveness, many of these militias are used as 'fire brigades'.

Asa'ib Ahl al-Haq
Largely consisting of former Iraqi Army and Police special forces operatives (trained by the US military in the 2000s), this unit originally deployed to Syria under IRGC auspices with about 1,000 fighters. After suffering significant losses during the first Iranian-led operations in 2012, it recovered during late 2013 and became the most important pro-Iranian asset in Syria, gaining much political influence in Iraq too.

Hezbollah Brigades
Established as an Iraqi Shi'a insurgent group in summer 2004, the **Kata'ib Hezbollah** fought the US presence in Iraq for years, resulting in it being declared a terrorist organisation by the USA. It deployed a battalion-sized group of combatants – led by an IRGC and Hezbollah cadre – to Rif Dimashq and as of late 2013 was responsible for the protection of Damascus IAP.

Kata'ib Sayyid ash-Shuhada
This 500-strong splinter group from Kata'ib Hezbollah is led by Mustafa Sheibani (holder of dual Iranian and Iraqi citizenship). It is usually deployed as infantry assigned to the RGD and saw much fighting in Western Ghouta, in 2013.

Promised Day Brigades (PDB)
This successor to Moqtada as-Sadr's **Army of Mahdi (Jaysh al-Mahdi)** and rival of the Asa'ib al-Haq group is the **Liwa al-Youm al-Mawud** of about 1,000 well-trained and experienced combatants in Syria. This unit seems to have closely co-operated with Hezbollah early in its deployment, while it has often since acted as mechanised infantry for what is left of the 4th AD of the Syrian military.

Sons of the Badr Brigade
The **Badr Corps (Failaq al-Badr)**, military wing of the Supreme Council for the Islamic Revolution in Iraq (originally established by Iraqi refugees in Iran in the early 1980s), became a political party and had many of its combatants joining the Iraqi Army in recent years. On instructions from Tehran, it established the 'Sons of the Badr Brigade' that has meanwhile deployed about 1,000 well-trained and experienced combatants in support of Assad's government in Syria.

Abu Fadl al-Abbas Brigade (LAFA)
The **Liwa Abu al-Fadl al-Abbas** was one of the first Iranian-sponsored units of Iraqi Shi'a to deploy inside Syria, and is thus the best known to the public. Counting about 1,500 fighters, initially it was primarily deployed for protection of the Sayida Zaynab Shrine, but following a number of clashes with various other Iraqi militias it was re-deployed to Damascus IAP.

Zulfiqar Brigade
The **Liwa al-Zulfiqar** was established in May and June 2013, partly from a cadre drafted from the LAFA and also from other Iraqi Shi'a militias, with the purpose of guarding the Sayida Zaynab Shrine and thus lessening tensions between rival Shi'a Iraqi groups in Syria.

The Praise Brigade

Established in July 2013, the **Liwa al-Ahmad** is another little-known group of Iranian-sponsored Iraqi Shi'a fighting in Syria, totalling perhaps 500 combatants.

Liwa Ammar Ibn Yassir

This brigade-sized force arrived in the Aleppo area in autumn 2013, since when it has been fighting in co-operation with Hezbollah, the NDF, and Liwa al-Zulfiqar.

Liwa al-Imam al-Hassan al-Mujtaba

This is another force of about 1,000 Iraqi Shi'a combatants recruited by Iranians, which emerged in Syria in early December 2013. According to unconfirmed reports, it was deployed to reinforce the garrison in Dayr az-Zawr, where it would have suffered significant losses.

Syrian Social Nationalist Party (SSNP)

The SSNP is a political party with long traditions and considerable influence in Lebanon and Syria since the 1940s. Once a fierce rival of the Ba'ath Party and Syrian Communist Party, it was practically wiped out as a political force in Syria during the 1960s but experienced a revival of sorts during the 1990s, and especially since Hafez al-Assad's succession by his son Bashar. Legalised in 2005, it become one of the largest political parties in the country, counting as many as 100,000 members, predominantly Christians. The SSNP established its own militia with support from the government and Iran, and is meanwhile operating about a dozen battalion-sized units, several of which are deployed on battlefields in Aleppo, while others are operating in the Qalamoun area and Homs Province.

Army of Monotheists (or Unitarians)

The Jaysh al-Muwahhideen is a Druze militant group of unknown size, established in early 2013 in Suwayda Province. It is fighting against insurgents and is de-facto for the government of Bashar al-Assad since late that year and early 2014, primarily in the Bosra area.

Palestine Liberation Army (PLA)

Set up as the supposed military wing of the PLO back in 1964, the PLA never came under the control of that organisation but developed into a proxy of the Syrian government. Trained and equipped by the SyAA, it was organised into three brigades that took part in the ill-fated Syrian intervention in Jordan in September 1970 and in the Lebanon War of the 1980s. While large parts of the PLA joined the Palestinian Authority's National Guard and returned to the 'Palestinian Territories' (West Bank and Gaza) in 1993, additional Palestinian refugees in Syria have since been drafted to rebuild this organisation. About 4,000 of them are presently fighting for the government in Damascus.

Popular Front for the Liberation of Palestine – General Command (PFLP-GC)

Founded in 1968, the PFLP-GC is a small Palestinian nationalist militant organisation based in Yarmuk Camp. Involved in numerous earlier attacks on Israel, it has been largely inactive since the late 1980s but remains designated a terrorist organisation by the US. When protesting reached Palestinian refugee camps in early June 2011, the government reacted by deploying its own troops, but also the PFLP, which resulted in a rift within the Palestinian ranks. While part of the PFLP opposed this alliance and resigned in protest, the majority sided with Bashar al-Assad and helped the military fight the insurgents. Ever since, many disaffected PFLP-GC combatants have defected to the insurgent side, where they established the Storm Brigade (Liwa al-Asifa), which is allied with the FSA and fighting in southern Syria.

Arab Nationalist Guards

This is a group of Egyptian, Iraqi, Palestinian and Syrian followers of Gamal Abdel Nasser's pan-Arabic ideas that declared themselves for 'military resistance movement operating in the Syrian Arab Republic, established in April 2013 to confront all Takfiri movements that aim to strike our unity and aim to sow divisions between Arabs'. Operating out of Sidon in Lebanon and closely co-operating with the NDF, its fighters are organised into four small battalions named after their fallen commanders: Wahid Haddad, Haydar al-Amali, Mohammed Brahmi and Jules Jammal. During late 2013 and early 2014, these have fought in Rif Dimashq, Dera'a, Homs and Aleppo, but primarily in the Qalamoun area.

Syrian Resistance (TSR)

The Muqawamat as-Suryah is a Marxist-Leninist gang of about 200 Turkish Alawites led by Mihrac Ural, a Turkish fugitive and former senior operator of Acilciler (splinter group from the terrorist organisation Turkish People's Party/Front), and who is still on the Interpol Red Notice list. It is only known for its activity in Tartous Province, where it became notorious for committing large-scale atrocities against Sunis in the Banias area.

Jihad instead of Revolution

With the memory of the West coming to the aid of a similar uprising in Libya in 2011 still fresh, and although not calling for a direct military intervention, many Syrian oppositionals were hoping to receive similar help in the form of arms, ammunition and supplies that would enable them to fight the government on equal terms. Instead, they got little but empty rhetoric and scant condemnations of atrocities committed by government forces. The consequences of this failure of Western politics are manifold and far-reaching, and nowhere near as clearly seen as from the transformation of the Syrian insurgency in 2013.

Instead of Western powers, Saudi Arabia, Qatar, Kuwait, Turkey and the United Arab Emirates stepped in and began providing aid to different insurgent groups, usually on condition that the groups in question emphasised their preferred ideology. Under their influence, most Syrian insurgents – the vast majority of whom used to be completely non-religious – began experiencing a radical change in their points of view. Concluding their earlier beliefs to be 'political idolatry', and the 'democracy' as propagated by the West for 'Western lies', many of them turned to Islamist ideology instead. While this resulted in a dramatic change of the ideological landscape of the Syrian insurgency, Syrians remain Syrians, despite the influence of foreign fundamentalists. Correspondingly, and despite countless feuds, the majority of insurgent groups continue co-operating with each other on the battlefield, emphasising the defeat of the government over political and religious ideology. Their primary aim remains the removal of Assad's government in Damascus, and most of them continue insisting that the political future of the country should be sorted out only once the war is over.

MAJOR INSURGENT UMBRELLA ORGANISATIONS

Moslem Brotherhood (MB)

The MB was not involved in the Syrian uprising of spring 2011, but its expatriated members became involved in searching for international support for it. Apart from creating the 'Commission for Civilian Protection' – tasked with connecting different FSA and SILF groups with sponsors abroad – and with extensive financial support from Qatar, they became dominant in the SNC and have gained control of nearly three-quarters of the units affiliated with the FSA. Although reportedly establishing their own militia (supposedly not affiliated with the FSA) – the Armed Men of the Moslem Brotherhood – the Moslem Brotherhood was not known to have appeared on the battlefields of the Syrian Civil War by late 2013.

Free Syrian Army

As of late 2013, the FSA remains the numerically largest insurgent organisation in Syria, totalling at least 35,000, perhaps as many as 60,000 combatants. It is still the dominant insurgent force in the Dera'a and Qunaitra Provinces, where it can reach back upon direct support from Saudi Arabia and Jordan. Its smaller units co-operate with other insurgent groups – primarily the IF – in Aleppo, Homs and Idlib Provinces, with the help of supplies flowing from Turkey. However, several of its units in north-eastern Syria have defected to the JAN, while others were subsequently destroyed by ISIS in 2013. Much of the FSA in this part of Syria now consists of smaller, local units that officially declare their allegiance but are foremost doing so in order to receive money and supplies from the SMC.

Syrian Islamic Front (SIF)

This was an umbrella organisation of Islamist and Salafist insurgents, founded on 21 December 2012, and including units like Ahrar ash-Sham, al-Haqq Brigade (Homs), al-Fajr Islamic Movement (Aleppo), Ansar ash-Sham (Lattakia), Jaysh al-Tawhid (Dayr az-Zawr) and the Hamza Ibn Abd al-Muttaib Brigade (Damascus). Some of the groups in question united with Ahrar ash-Sham in early 2013, while a few other Salafist units united as the Liwa Mujahidi ash-Sham. In November 2013, the SIF joined the newly-created Islamic Front.

Syrian Islamic Liberation Front (SILF)

The SILF was formed in September 2013 as an umbrella for 20 Islamic-motivated insurgent groups, including Suqour ash-Sham Brigade (Idlib), Farouq Brigade (Homs), Liwa al-Islam and Tajamo Ansar al-Islam (Damascus), Tawhid Brigade and Amb Ibn al-Aas Brigade (Aleppo), al-Nasser Salahaddin Brigade (Latakia) and Liwa Dawoud. The ideology of the SILF was based on Sunni Islam, with minimalist political aims, except for a declaration that Sharia law was its point of reference and promising protection of minorities. While some SILF groups were declaring themselves to be allied with both the FSA and the SILF, and this umbrella organisation included MB and Salafist-inspired groups, the Ahrar ash-Sham Brigade distanced itself from it, and the SILF was generally not co-operating with the JAN. Eventually, the SILF was disbanded in November 2013 and most of its structure and units have joined the Islamic Front.

Brigade of Islam/Army of Islam

The **Liwa al-Islam** was established by a group of Salafists freshly released from government prisons in early 2012 and became the driving force behind most insurgent operations in Damascus and Eastern Ghouta during that year. Reinforced through Saudi support (in order to create a counterpart for the JAN), in November 2013 it was expanded through the inclusion of about 60 different insurgent groups into the Army of Islam (Jaysh al-Islam), which is active in Eastern Ghouta. The **Jaysh al-Islam** has been co-operating with the JAN and many other insurgent groups (including Christian and Druze formations), and is presently operating some of the best and most sophisticated weapons systems in the insurgent arsenal. This includes two L-39ZOs (which appear not to have been used in combat so far), two 9K33 Osa/SA-13 SAM systems (one of which was deployed to shoot down a SyAAF Mi-8 over Damascus in November 2013) and a company of T-72AV MBTs (bought from the commander of one of 4th AD's units).

Islamic Front (IF)

The **al-Jabhat al-Islamiyyah** is a coalition of seven major insurgent groups – including Ahrar ash-Sham, Suqour ash-Sham (Idlib), Liwa al-Tawhid (Aleppo), Jaysh al-Islam (Damascus), Liwa al-Haqq (Homs), Ansar ash-Sham and the Kurdish Islamic Front – established on 22 November 2013. It totals up to 45,000 combatants primarily active in Idlib, Aleppo, Hama and Homs Provinces. Its leadership does not maintain ties with the SNC, and some of its units have meanwhile confiscated most of the property of FSA units destroyed by ISIS. The IF is generally co-operating with the JAN, and some of its elements either used to co-operate, or still co-operate, with ISIS. However, units operating in Aleppo and Idlib have launched a major offensive that resulted in the wholesale collapse of the Wahhabist establishment in these two provinces in early 2014.

Southern Front & Syria Revolutionaries Front (SRF)

This is an alliance of 14 'moderate' insurgent brigades created in December 2013 with Saudi support, though in reaction to the emergence of the Islamic Front. Although the groups in question used to operate within the FSA framework (indeed, some of its groups – like the former Shuhada Jebel az-Zawiya Battalion, later Syrian Martyrs Brigade; then Idlib Martyrs Brigade and the Idlib Military Council – were among the first ever FSA units), they are no longer affiliated with it. Led by wealthy businessman Bashar al-Zoubi, who maintains excellent contacts with Saudi Arabia, the Southern Front was highly successful in southern Syria in late 2013 and early 2014. Led by Jamal Maarouf, the SRF was badly hampered by lack of supplies and heavy losses caused by SyAAF air strikes in 2013, but this began to change in early 2014, when they started receiving aid from Saudi Arabia too. According to its leaders, these two organisations might have up to 30,000 fighters in the south and up to 18,000 in northern Syria. They are at war with the government and ISIS, and their leaders are sought after by the JAN.

MAJOR INSURGENT COMBAT UNITS

Farouq Brigades

The original Farouq Battalion was established by Army defectors in Homs in June 2011 as a sub-unit of the Khalid Ibn al-Wallid Brigade. After suffering heavy casualties during the siege of Bab Amr, it was forced to withdraw into Rastan and Qusayr, where it was reorganised and expanded through absorbing various minor insurgent units. In 2012 the Farouq Brigades spread their influence into Dera'a Province, and then joined the Suqour ash-Sham to establish the SILF. Islamist by orientation, the Farouq Brigades now have about 15,000 combatants and are co-operating with the Islamic Front. This movement has lost all elements that used to operate under FSA command in northern Syria during feuds with Ahrar ash-Sham, JAN and ISIS in late 2013 – and, consequently, much of its influence.

Grandsons of the Prophet Brigade

Totalling about 15,000 combatants supported by the Qatari government, the **Ahfad ar-Rasul Brigade** is one of the largest independent insurgent formations in Syria. Primarily active in Idlib and Aleppo, it actively co-operates with the FSA, and in late 2013 and early 2104 proved instrumental in destroying ISIS's presence in these provinces.

Islamic Movement of the Free Men of the Levant

The Harakat **Ahrar ash-Sham** al-Islami came into being as a coalition of 25 Islamist and Salafist units from Idlib Province, totalling about 13,000 fighters in July 2013. Many of its founders were political prisoners released in 2011. Led by Hassan Aboud, this powerful formation gained influence controlling more than 80 units operational in Aleppo, Idlib and Hama. Ahrar ash-Sham operates a number of well-armed and -supplied – motorised and mechanised units that often co-operate with the FSA and other insurgent groups, but does not maintaing ties with the SNC. While previously co-operating with ISIS – and still in the Dayr az-Zawr area – it has been on a war footing against Wahhabists around Aleppo since late 2013.

Falcons of the Levant Brigade

Largely consisting of defected SyAA officers and other ranks, the **Suqour ash-Sham** (or Sham Falcons Brigade) came into being as part of the FSA in the Jabal az-Zawiya region of Idlib Province in September 2011. By 2012, it was one of the best armed and most active insurgent groups, participating in several large-scale offensives in Idlib, Hama, Lattakia and Aleppo. Although initially recognising the SNC, in late 2013 it declared itself independent from the FSA. Subsequently the Suqour ash-Sham joined other Islamist organisations to establish the SIF (this alliance was superseded in November 2013 by the IF, which is still led by the Suqour ash-Sham Brigade's leader, Abu Issa), and in early 2014 became involved in a major offensive against ISIS.

Dawoud Brigade

One of the major elements of the Suqour ash-Sham Brigades is the Liwa al-Dawoud. Established in spring 2012 in the Sarmin area (eastern Idlib Province), it developed into a relatively effective formation of about 1,500 insurgents. In December 2013, its leader Hassan Aboud (not to be mixed with Hassan Abboud of Harakar Ahrar ash-Sham) announced his intention to join ISIS, but this caused resistance, defections and even infighting within the brigade. The rest of Suqour ash-Sham overran the part of Liwa al-Dawoud that attempted to join ISIS in Sarqib in mid-January 2014.

Unity Brigade

Created through the merger of the Fursan al-Jabal, Daret Izza and Ahrar ash-Shamal Brigades, the Qatar-supported **Liwa al-Tawhid** was established with the intention of better co-ordinating insurgent operations in Aleppo City, and developed into the most powerful insurgent formation in that part of Syria, totalling about 3,000 well-equipped and trained fighters. Although announcing its support for the SNC, it joined the SILF in January 2013, and is meanwhile a part of the IF.

Banner of the Nation Brigades

The **Liwaa al-Umma** is an insurgent group established by Mahdi al-Harati, an Irish-Libyan leader of the revolution in Libya, in early 2012. While about 90 percent of its 6,000 combatants are Syrians, it includes Libyans, Egyptians, Palestinians and other Arabs. Funded by private donations from Libya, Kuwait and Turkey, since September 2012 Liwa al-Umma is aligned with the FSA and fighting in Aleppo and Homs.

Syrian Turkmen Brigades

This is no solid block, but a number of minor groups and units, usually allied with the FSA but also other insurgent groups, established by Syrian Turkmen in Aleppo, Homs, Lattakia and elsewhere, totalling about 10,000 combatants.

Army of Mujahedeen

Numbering about 6,000 fighters, the **Jaysh al-Mujahedeen** is another group that separated from the FSA. It was established in late 2013 as a coalition of three FSA brigades (including the 'Division 19') in the Aleppo area, with the primary purpose of fighting ISIS.

Jabhat al-Assala wa'Tanmia

The Jabhat al-Assala wa'Tanmia is an organisation established in late 2013 with funding from private sources in Saudi Arabia and Kuwait, which intended to establish a 'moderate' Salafist and Wahhabist counterpart to ISIS. Consisting of Syrian and foreign combatants, it is deployed in Aleppo and co-operates with other insurgent groups, but fights ISIS.

Strangers of the Region of Syria

The **Ghuraba ash-Sham** was a group of about 2,000 secularists and Islamists that emerged in 2012, favouring a non-religious state, but which got involved in looting and – at times – collaborating with the government, and was dispersed in the course of clashes with fundamentalist groups in May 2013. After being practically disarmed in November 2013, and having its commander, Ghuraba ash-Sham, publicly executed by ISIS in the town of Atareb, it nearly disappeared. Its remaining 100 fighters are include a 'battalion' largely made up of women, but their overall combat effectiveness is nearly non-existent.

Jabahat an-Nusra (JAN)

The Support Front for the People of Levant by the Levantine Mujaheddin on the Battlefields of Jihad (Jabhat an-Nusra il-Ahl ash-Sham min Mujahedi ash-Sham fi Sahat al-Jihad, usually shortened to an-Nusra Front, Jabhat an-Nusra or JAN) emerged in early 2012 as an organisation of Syrian Salafists, led by Abu Muhammad al-Jawlani.[34] Established in the Damascus area, JAN pledged allegiance to al-Qaida's mastermind Ayman Mohammad Rabie al-Zawahiri – which resulted in this organisation promptly ending up on the USA's list of terrorist organisations. With plentiful financial support from al-Qaida, JAN grew in numbers and moved its centre of operations to north-eastern Syria, where it co-operated with local Salafist clans, but foremost ISIL in Iraq (see below for details). JAN grew to about 15,000 fighters, the majority of whom are Syrians. A few smaller groups are active in Dera'a and the Qalamoun Range, but most are deployed along the Euphrates River, where they established themselves in control through 2013. The movement co-operates with nearly all existing insurgent groups, including Christians and Turkmen, and repeatedly declared having no intentions of waging a 'global Jihad'. Some JAN units – especially those deployed in the Dayr az-Zawr area, like Tajamu Mujahidee al-Qaqaa, Liwa al-Qaqaa and Kataeb Allahu Akbar –still co-operate with ISIS, but others openly rebelled against the Wahhabists, often with dire consequences for their commanders. A classic example was the Jabhat ar-Raqqa an-Nusra Brigade, which captured ar-Raqqa only to be destroyed by ISIS in September 2013.

The Green Battalion

This is a group of primarily Saudi Jihadists, with a small Syrian component, which appeared in the Qalamoun area in September 2013. While co-operating with ISIS and JAN, it insisted on independence from both because of personal differences between different leaders.

Harakat Sham al-Islam

Founded and led by Moroccans, this group participated in the Lattakia offensive in summer 2013, and has since been fighting in alliance with JAN in the Aleppo area.

Saraya Marwan Hadid

This is a company-sized outfit of fundamentalist Lebanese Sunni, established in December 2012 with the purpose of 'defending Lebanese Sunnis from invasion of the Party of Iran' (meaning Hezbollah). The group went into action in June the same year by launching a few BM-21 rockets at the Hezbollah-held Beka'a Valley. The group subsequently crossed the border to Syria to join the Abdullah Azzam Brigades of JAN, operational in the Qalamoun Range.

Fighting Their Own War, Part 1: Wahhabists

Because of their black flags and Islam-motivated insignia, the fundamentalist Syrian insurgent groups visually resemble what is colloquially known as 'Jihadists': Islamist extremists waging a global 'holy war' against any 'infidels'. Indeed, there are several armed groups of native Syrians, and several groups of foreigners affiliated with al-Qaida, present in the country. However, a closer look at their origins, organisation, ideology and activities reveals that their total numbers are far fewer than those of genuine insurgents, and that most of them hardly ever became involved in fighting the Syrian government.

The Islamic State of Iraq and the Levant (ISIL/ISIS)

This Jihadist group was originally established as The Organisation of Monotheism and Jihad, in Iraq in early 2004. After merging with several smaller groups it evolved into The Islamic State of Iraq and the Levant (ISIL), colloquially known as 'al-Qaida in Iraq'. ISIL began financially supporting JAN and then infiltrating over the border into Syria through bribing the remaining government authorities in the Dayr az-Zawr area in 2012. In April 2013, ISIL's leader, Abu Bakr al-Baghdadi, announced a merger of his organisation with JAN into the ad-Dawla al-Islamiyya fi al-Iraq wa-sh-Sham (The Islamic Sate of Iraq and Syria, ISIS). The merger was strongly rejected by JAN, and then by al-Qaida's mastermind, Ayman Mohammad Rabie al-Zawahiri. JAN chief al-Jawlani insisted on his organisation being interested in defeating the government and establishing an Islamic state in Syria, not waging a global Jihad. Knowing about ISIL's ferocious reputation from Iraq – based on hundreds of suicide attacks, bestial summary executions and abuse of human rights – Al-Zawahiri understood the sensitiveness of the Wahhabist presence in Syria and negative repercussions from the spread of their terror. His concerns proved correct when ISIS – insisting on the establishment of an Islamic caliphate in majority Sunni populated regions of Iraq and Syria, and hardly ever involved in operations against the government in Damascus – launched a campaign of terror and destruction against native insurgents, opponents and activists.

For much of 2013, ISIS and JAN maintained a complex structure of co-operation, depending on local circumstances and relations. They were strictly separated in the Aleppo and Damascus areas, but closely co-operated in Hassaka, Raqqa (where the local ISIS unit defected to JAN in July 2013 in protest over Jihadi misconduct against native insurgent groups and Syrians in general) and Dayr az-Zawr, while only JAN is present in the Dera'a Province and Qalamoun Range. Although including a small number of Syrians, ISIS is led and dominated by foreign Jihadists, including about 8,000 (US and Israeli sources cite up to 30,000) Iraqis, Chechens, Libyans, Egyptians, Saudis, Tunisians and significant numbers of Islamist extremists from the West.

It was in this way that an ironic situation came into being: because media reporting about the civil war is nowadays dominated by coverage of Islamist fundamentalists, an image was created of the government of Bashar al-Assad facing exactly the kind of armed opposition – namely 'bearded men with extreme religious beliefs', an 'invasion by CIA-supported al-Qaida' – which it was claiming to be facing since the first protests in Dera'a. For many foreign observers, this is 'a matter of fact', and there is plenty of ignorance of the fact that it was Assad's government that applied brutal force with great acumen right from the start of peaceful protesting, in turn provoking the civil war; that ISIS became involved in less than a handful of operations against the government in Damascus; and that it established itself in control of much of north-eastern Syria through pursuing the strategy of destroying native insurgents. As such, ISIS is no 'armed resistance group', or one that is bringing ever larger insurgent groups under its control, but a foreign body tarnishing the image of the Syrian revolution and running a campaign of destroying the Syrian insurgency.

In order to establish an image of a 'native' and 'popular' movement, but also for the purpose of better battlefield control, ISIS has established a number of front groups in Aleppo, Idlib and Lattakia Provinces. The best known of these are as follows:

Northern Group/Jaysh al-Muharijeen wa al-Ansar (JMWA)

This is the most prominent Jihadist group in Syria, led by Omar ash-Shishani, veteran intelligence officer of the Georgian Army of Chechen origin. Nearly always declared as a 'separate group' and no part of ISIS, the JMWA used to represent ISIS in Aleppo and Raqqa Provinces in 2013, but also maintained branches present in Idlib and Lattakia. This group split between those who insist on remaining with ISIS and ash-Shihani's group that joined JAN in November 2013. The part that remained with ISIS suffered heavy losses during the insurgent offensive in early 2014, and practically disappeared from parts of Syria west of Kweres AB.

Lions of the Caliphate Battalion

Led by Egyptian Abu Muadh al-Masry, this is an 'elite' fighting force of ISIS: a well-trained and equipped SWAT-type asset that was primarily active in the Qalamoun area. While earlier co-operating with some insurgent groups, since its joint attack on Dayr Attiyeh with ISIS in November 2013, it was openly hostile even to JAN but has not ben heard of since.

Jamiat Jund ash-Sham

This group of primarily Lebanese Jihadists has been active in the Homs and northern Rif Dimashq Provinces since August 2013. While hostile to most other native insurgent groups, it co-operates with JAN and was lately active in the Qalamoun area.

Jund Allah Brigade in Bilad ash-Sham

This was the ISIS front responsible for spreading its influence into Idlib and Hama Provinces. It established itself in control of Ma'arat an-Numaan in early 2013 through violence, suppression of any kind of opposition and countless executions of leading opponents. It was largely destroyed during the insurgent counteroffensive of early 2014, and its present status is unclear.

Suqur al-Ezz

This was another group of primarily Saudi Jihadists with personal problems with ISIS and JAN that used to be active in the Aleppo area.

Habib al-Mustafa Brigades

This small group of Iraqi Salafists from Falluja was largely destroyed during fighting around Dayr az-Zawr in December 2013.

Fighting Their Own War, Part 2: Kurds and Assyrians

Kurds have traditionally suffered a lot under the Assad government and their cautious behaviour since the start of this war is mirroring their painful experiences from the past. Kurds were swift to organise armed militias and bring sizeable portions of northern and north-eastern Syria – including predominantly

Kurdish-populated parts of Aleppo – under their control.

Out of about a dozen different Kurdish political parties in Syria, the Democratic Union Party (Partiya Yekitiya Demokrat, PYD) – established in 2003 and affiliated with the Kurdistan Worker's Party (PKK) that used to wage insurgency inside Turkey – emerged as the strongest. What levels of popularity the PYD actually enjoys is unclear, but it is a well-organised structure with enough influence to perform quasi-governmental roles.

Insisting on guarantying Kurdish rights and security, the PYD established its own military wing, the People's Protection Units (Yekineyen Parastina Gel, YPG), which was expanded into the official armed wing of the Kurdish Supreme Committee, a governing body of Syrian Kurdistan established in July 2012. Due to support from Iraqi Kurds and elsewhere, the YPG developed as a well-trained and armed, disciplined force that maintains a defensive position. Generally, it holds areas predominantly populated by Kurds and seldom ventures outside: although involved in a few clashes with insurgents and government forces, it launched major military operations only against the extremists of ISIS in the Hassaka and ar-Raqqa Provinces, starting in mid-July 2013.

Although sometimes co-operating with various insurgent factions, Kurds appear not to be eager to get involved in the war against the government. The YPG tolerates the government's presence in Hassaka and Qamishli, while controlling the Rumeilan refinery and earning profits from selling oil to the government through the Homs and Shadada pipelines. On the other hand, the PYD/YPG conglomerate has created the Jabhat al-Akrad militia in Aleppo Province, a Kurdish force fighting the regime and openly co-operating with most insurgent factions in this part of Syria.

YPG

Jabhat al-Akrad

Syriac Military Council

The Mawtbo Fulhoyo Suryoyo is a self-defence organisation of Assyrian Christians in eastern Hassaka Province. Established in early 2013 in co-operation with the PYD/YPG, it recruited about 1,500 armed men and women who have seen some limited action against ISIS in the Tel Hamis area in late 2013 and early 2014, but otherwise primarily man various checkpoints.

Notes

1. As is well-known, the British subsequently enthroned Faisal as King of Iraq, and his brother Abdullah I Ibn al-Hussein as Emir of Transjordan (since 1946, King of Jordan). It is less well-known that the British then went on to leave Sharif Hussein to his own devices when he came under attack by Abdul-Aziz Ibn al-Saud, the ruler from the neighbouring Nejd region, in 1924, who subsequently established the Kingdom of Saudi Arabia. Furthermore, contrary to widespread belief (and the behaviour of French Mandate authorities), Syria was never a French 'colony'. Finally, it is next to unknown that in 1919 Faisal met Dr Chaim Weizman, the head of the Zionist Commission of Palestine, and reached an agreement about full co-operation in the development of an independent Arab state. This agreement encouraged 'the immigration of Jews into Palestine on large scale' and 'as quickly as possible', but also stressed that, 'Arab peasant and tenant farmers shall be protected in their rights and shall be assisted in forwarding their economic development'. This agreement accepted the much-cited Balfour Declaration and the development of a Jewish home in Palestine – but this was to become a part of one, Arab state, ruled 'by the most cordial goodwill and understanding, and to this end Arab and Jewish duly accredited agents' (see text of the 'Agreement between Emir Feisal and Dr Weizmann', from 3 January 1919). Tragically, as much as they ignored the findings for the King-Crane Commission, various subsequent leaders preferred to completely ignore this agreement, in turn provoking the Arab-Israeli conflict which – together with all of its negative consequences (including the spread of international terrorism and Islamic extremism) – is raging still nearly 90 years later.
2. As of 1955, the Chief of Syrian Military Intelligence found that approximately 65 percent of the NCOs belonged to the Alawi sect, see van Dam, *The Struggle for Power in Syria*, pp26–28.
3. Baer, *The Saudi Connection*, pp151–155.
4. According to Syrian sources, no less than 10 Israeli UAVs were shot down by the SyAAF over Syria on average every year between 2001 and 2006, principally while flying along the Syrian-Jordanian and Syrian-Turkish borders, but sometimes as deep as 50km inside Syrian airspace. The first shoot-down occurred in late July 2001, and the last known – a MiG-23ML downing a UAV armed with air-to-air missiles – in October 2007. The worst incident occurred on 14 September 2001, when – according to sources within the Syrian diaspora – two IDF/AF F-15s shot down two SyAAF MiG-29s off the Syrian coast, after the latter approached an Israeli intelligence-gathering aircraft. Such reports are denied by sources with links to British military intelligence, which stressed that no corresponding activity was observed by Royal Air Force radar stations at British bases on Cyprus.
5. According to Syrian sources, TURMS-T-equipped T-72M1s were locally designated 'T-82'; similarly, T-72AVs were locally designated 'T-74'.
6. Much of Syria's BM-21 stocks were imported from Egypt, while the first confirmed deployment of BM-27 systems took place in early 2014.
7. 'The Sturdy House That Assad Built', *Foreign Affairs*, March 2011.
8. Initially, officers from the 65th MB complained to their superiors about misbehaviour of a number of leading officers, torture and execution of civilians, looting and cases of raped women. When officers reporting such misbehaviour were arrested instead, they began searching for a way out.
9. Among officers who defected was 1st Lt Abdul Razzaq Tlass, nephew of Mustafa Tlass, who left the 65th MB and managed to reach ar-Rastan together with many soldiers from this company. Together with defectors from the Homs area, he was to establish one of the first units of the future Free Syrian Army in mid-June 2011.
10. SANA release, 30 April 2011.
11. Presence of a company of Quds operatives was reported in Dera'a in April 2011, where they were advising security forces, lending their experiences from crushing similar mass protests in Iran in 2009.
12. Syrian media reported the death of at least 370 'members of security forces' by 5 June 2011. Although some of these were actually victims of summary executions by intelligence operatives, snipers and superior officers, several dozen were killed during the fighting for Jisr ash-Shugor.
13. The first large-scale massacres occurred in May 2011, when pro-government militias stabbed or shot at close range at least 108 Sunni residents of Taldou, in the Houleh area of Homs Province. Less than two weeks later, militias murdered another 100 Sunnis in Qubeir, in Hama Province, including 40 women and children.
14. Although – except for SANA releases – no official documentation is available, anecdotes from reporters visiting various military hospitals in Damascus and Homs during this period seem to reinforce conclusions about very heavy losses of government forces. Furthermore, a video from an Alawite wedding posted on YouTube showed Lt Gen Ali Khouzam explaining to young men that only three members of a 50-man RGD company remained alive after an attack on Bab Amr (Khouzam was killed just a few days later).
15. As well as killing and injuring dozens of loyalist troops, the insurgents have assassinated or captured a significant number of top commanders, including Maj Gen Faraq Shehada, Commander I Corps SyAA.
16. Rajiha was replaced by Lt Gen Fahd Jassim al-Furayj, former Chief of Staff Armed Forces.
17. Exact numbers of casualties on all sides of this battle remain unknown. The government ceased the practice of reporting its official casualty figures via SANA releases in June 2012, when it became obvious that the nature of the situation had changed fundamentally and it could no longer maintain its narrative about facing a 'small-scale terrorist conspiracy'. By that time, the Syrian government admitted to have suffered more than 2,300 killed, of whom 75 percent were military personnel, and the rest police, intelligence operatives and civil servants, primarily Alawites from Lattakia and Homs Provinces.
18. Notable is that the correct translation of the modern-day SyAAF's designation from Arabic ends with the word 'Forces', plural, because the SyAAF is meanwhile including the former Air Defence Force.
19. Only the designations of two operational divisions are known, the 21st and 22nd, but it remains unknown for what part of Syrian airspace which of these was responsible, or whether they remain current.
20. Data about the number of Mi-8/17s and Mi-25s in service with the SyAAF according to Brig Gen Mohammad al-Zogby and Brig Gen Saed Shawamra, who defected from Taftanaz AB in June 2012.
21. This is the major reason for the use of plural 'Forces' in the official SyAAF title.

22. The division in question used to be numbered the 24th, but it is unknown whether this designation remains current.

23. Syria originally purchased 20 Su-24MKs, starting in 1987. One crashed in the 1990s, but two – one Su-24MK and one Su-24MR electronic-reconnaissance fighter – were donated by Libya in exchange for maintenance support of the former Libyan Arab Air Force in spite of an international arms embargo. Reportedly, up to 10 SyAAF Su-24s were still in Russia as of autumn 2012, but Syrians and Russians subsequently 'found the ways to return them home'.

24. Among leading defectors were Brig Gen Mohammed Fares, the first Syrian kosmonaut, and Deputy Director AFI for Dayr az-Zawr, Brig Gen Mustafa Nassr.

25. This précis of vehicles lost during the break-out from Bab al-Hawa is provided to illustrate the colourful composition of Syrian military units at this time, caused by frequent reshuffling of company-sized detachments from one unit to the other in order to prevent defections.

26. Although much of the SyAAF personnel remain loyal to the government, and despite stringent control by the AFI and other intelligence agencies, there are a significant number of sympathisers who maintain contact with the insurgency and sometimes provide valuable intelligence. It was in this way that the orders from Ba'ath Party's HQ were revealed to the public, but also that – in combination with monitoring and reporting of the air force's operations – the quite detailed statistics about the number of combat sorties flown by SyAAF presented here became available. Furthermore, it is notable that while obeying their orders some of the pilots are purposely missed their targets or re-set fuses of their weapons so that they failed to detonate.

27. On 15 October, the HQ FSA released a report according to which the insurgents had shot down no less than 71 military aircraft –27 MiGs and Sukhois and 44 helicopters – of which 57 have been documented by photographs and videos. However, evidence published by this and other insurgent sources by the end of that month confirmed only the downing of 14 jets and 16 helicopters. Arguably, up to 20 additional jets were destroyed on the ground, but these included MiG-21s and MiG-23s that were withdrawn from service years earlier and only used as decoys.

28. Although known as a 'camp', Yarmuk was officially established in 1957 to provide an informal and largely tended area for Palestinians who fled after Israel's foundation in 1948. It is a built-up, urban area, with apartment blocks, shops, schools and hospitals.

29. Although the THK had a total of 18 RF-4s upgraded to ETM standard (17 were in service with 113th and 173rd Squadrons as of 22 June 2012), this was one of only two examples capable of carrying the KS-146 LOROP reconnaissance pod (the other one is 77-0316). With the THK conducting ELINT/SIGINT operations with other types in service, its RF-4ETMs are equipped only with the AN/ALQ-178/(V)3 radar-warning-receivers. Bodies of the two crew members were recovered in early July 2012.

30. The Turkish Air Force 'avenged' the loss of its RF-4 on 16 September 2013, when two Lockheed F-16C interceptors from 181 Filo (No. 181 Squadron) intercepted a SyAAF Mi-17 helicopter nearly 10 kilometres inside Turkish airspace, over Yayladag Gendarmerie Post in Hatay Province, and shot it down after it failed to react to repeated warnings, around 2:27 p.m. local time. At least two crew members managed to jump out of the burning helicopter before it hit the ground. After landing inside Turkey, they managed to run over the border into Syria but were captured by extremist Islamists of ISIS and summarily executed shortly after.

31. Overall, such 'mishaps' should have resulted in Hezbollah suffering at least 28 KIA (in addition to eight officers from the Quds Force). According to Hezbollah sources (interviews provided on condition of anonymity, January 2014), even the problem with the SyAAF was only solved through, 'deployment of pilots that were no [sic] Syrians'.

32. While Iranian sources largely refused to comment in this regards, the above-mentioned Hezbollah and several insurgent sources indicate that the IRGC might have deployed several of its own Mi-17 helicopters to Syria, and that its personnel are flying some of the SyAAF MiG-23s and MiG-29s. The IRGCASF is not operating these types in Iran but has pilots trained on fast jets, like Sukhoi Su-25s. Furthermore, considering Turkish military reports about a 'surge' in SyAAF training activities (reportedly, it was flying up to 50 training sorties a day during the second half of 2013) and a number of videos that appeared on YouTube during October 2013 (showing unarmed L-39s, MiG-23UBs and MiG-29UBs while returning to various bases), it is perfectly possible that the IRGCASF has re-qualified a number of its pilots to fly Syrian MiG-23s and MiG-29s.

33. Information according to Iranian sources, provided on condition of anonymity. The same have indicated that the helicopters in question were not operated by the SyAAF, but differ in regards of the number of IRGC operatives killed, some citing 10 and others 24. Videos provided by insurgent sources have shown three Mi-8s and Mi-17s as destroyed on or around 15–16 November 2013, two of these in the Aleppo area.

34. Although often bunched together with more militant Wahhabism, Salafism is a different fundamentalist belief, stressing a return to pure and authentic Islam. Salafists are generally apolitical, emphasising attempts to imitate the Prophet Mohammed and his companions by practicing their faith as closely as they can. The majority of Syrian Salafists ridiculed early calls for 'Jihad in Syria' issued by various Wahhabist theologics, and initially refused to have any links with them, which is why most Syrian Salafists joined organisations like Ahrar ash-Sham. In comparison, Wahhabism is the most radical and militant interpretation of Sunni Islam. Insisting on strict religious purity, this teaching emphasises doctrines and practices that are supposedly linked to early Islam, but meanwhile have next to no connection to it. Wahhabism was initiated by Muhammad Ibn Abd al-Wahhab from Nejd in the 18th Century. Wahhab was strongly influenced by the Koranic literalism of Ahmad Ibn Hanbal (who felt that Islam was overrun by corruption, superstition and extistentialism), and by the teachings of Islamic law scholar Taqi ad-Din Ahmad Ibn Taymiyyah. Ibn Taymiyyah's teachings were coloured by Crusader expeditions and the destruction of the Islamic Empire by Mongol invasions. He concluded that the reason for the collapse of this empire were authorities and political leaders who had failed to uphold the 'correct' ideals of Islam, and demanded 'true' Moslems to revolt against these leaders and help establish a 'proper' Islamic state. Following that example, Wahhab's teachings became so intolerant that he was forced to flee from one place to another before, in 1740, he found refugee in Diriyah, near Riyadh, which at that time was under the control of Muhammad Ibn Saud. Saud embraced Wahhab's ideas and they reached an agreement according to which the latter was to implement and enforce such teachings in exchange for Wahhab's recognition of Saud as the leader of the movement. For the following 140 years, the two families worked closely together to wage a series of wars, in the course of which they established themselves in control of what became the Kingdom of Saudi Arabia, in which Wahhabism is the state religion, indoctrinated in schools. Nevertheless, this movement began distancing itself from al-Sauds before the June 1967 Arab-Israeli War when – intent on countering Israel – Saudi royals launched a campaign of spreading Wahhabism outside the country. Using their oil wealth, they began establishing a network of charitable organisations and financing the development of new mosques and religious schools where a new generation of young, religiously motivated fighters was indoctrinated. In this fashion, Taymiyyah's and Wahhab's teachings became strongly influential in the emergence of modern-day fundamentalist and radical Islamist movements around the world.

Bibliography

Researching and reporting about an ongoing military conflict is never a pleasant task because – for obvious reasons – many of details about military operations are kept secret, and are going to remain that way for a while longer.

Much of the materials presented in this book were obtained in the course of research for the book series 'Arab MiGs', which presents the history of Arab air forces at war with Israel in the period 1955–1973. Additional information was acquired during interviews with participants and eyewitnesses, primarily in Syria, but also in Egypt, Libya, France, USA and Iraq. Sadly, differing threats for the security of specific people prevented most of them from speaking openly. Much additional information was compiled with help of visitors to the ACIG.info forum, who joined their efforts in attempting to follow developments in Syria as closely as possible. Contributions of all people who shared their insights proved precious and enabled me to cross-examine the following publications (as well as those mentioned in footnotes) that were consulted in the preparation of this book:

Baer, R., *Die Saudi-Connection* (C. Bertelsmann, 2004); German issue of *The Saudi-Connection*, (Santa Barbara: Random House, 2000). ISBN 3-570-00807-X

Barr, J., *A Line In the Sand: Britain, France and the Struggle That Shaped the Middle East* (London: Simon & Schuster UK Ltd, 2011). ISBN 978-1-84739-457-6

Blanford, N., 'The Battle for Qusayr: How the Syrian Regime and Hizb Allah Tipped the Balance', *CTC Sentinel*, Special Issue, Vol. 6/Issue 8 (West Point, 2013).

Cooper, T., Nicolle, D., with Nordeen, L., Salti, P. and Smisek, M., *Arab MiGs Volume 4: Attrition War, 1967–1973* (Houston: Harpia Publishing, 2013). ISBN 978-0-9854554-1-5

Exum, Andrew, *Hizballah at War: A Military Assessment* (The Washington Institute for Near East Policy, 2006).

Holliday, J., *The Assad Regime: From Counterinsurgency to Civil War* (Washington: Institute for the Study of War, 2013).

Holliday, J., *The Syrian Army: Doctrinal Order of Battle* (Washington: Institute for the Study of War, 2013).

Konzelmann, G., *Damaskus: Oase Zwischen Hass und Hoffnung* (Frankfurt/Main: Ulstein Buch, 1996). ISBN 3-548-35588-9

Mustafa, K., *The Fall of the Golan* (in Arabic) (Cairo: Dar al-Itisam, 1990).

Nassief, I., *The Campaign for Homs and Aleppo: The Assad Regime's Strategy in 2013* (Washington: Institute for the Study of War, 2014).

Nicolle, Dr D., *Crusader Warfare: Muslims, Mongols and the Struggle Against the Crusades* (Oxford: Osprey Publishing Ltd, 1998). ISBN 1-85532-697-3

Nicolle, Dr D., *Crusader Castles in the Holy Land 1192–1302*, (Oxford: Osprey Publishing Ltd, 2005). ISBN 1-84176-827-8

Provence, M., *The Great Syrian Revolt and the Rise of Arab Nationalism* (Austin: University of Texas Press, 2005). ISBN 0-292-70680-4

Razoux, P., *La Guerre des Six Jours (5–10 juin 1967): Du mythe à la réalité* (Paris: Economica, 2006). ISBN 978-2717851939

Stafrace, C., *Arab Air Forces* (Carrolton: Squadron/Signal Publications Inc., 1994). ISBN 0-89747-326-4

Szybala, V., *Assad Strikes Damascus: The Battle for Syria's Capital* (Washington, Institute for the Study of War, 2014).

Van Dam, N., *The Struggle for Power in Syria: Politics and Society Under Assad and the Ba'th Party* (I.B. Tauris, 1996). ISBN 978-1860640247

By All Means Necessary: Individual and Command Responsibility for Crimes against Humanity in Syria (Human Rights Watch, 2011). ISBN 1-56432-842-2

Hezbollah Operatives Killed in Syria (The Meir Amit Intelligence and Terrorism Information Center, 2013).

The History of the Syrian Army (in Arabic), (Damascus: Centre for Military Studies, 2001–2002).

Tanks of the World: Taschenbuch der Panzer (Koblenz: Bernard & Graefe Verlag, 1990). ISBN 3-7637-5871-2

Various magazines and journals published by the Syrian Ministry of Defence, 1980s, 1990s, and 2000s; interviews with dozens of Algerian, Egyptian, Iraqi, Syrian and Soviet Air Force officers, pilots and ground personnel.

Data about the number of Mi-8/17s and Mi-25s in service with the SyAAF according to Brig Gen Mohammad al-Zogby and Brig Gen Saed Shawamra, who defected from Taftanaz AB in June 2012.